Narcissism Rising! The Final World Empire

Narcissism Rising! The Final World Empire

A PROPHETIC PERSPECTIVE

Lori Buelow

Indy Pub

Dedication

This book is dedicated to the faithful and the many "Watchmen and Watchwomen" who have sounded the alarm about the Soon Return of Jesus and those events to come under The Final World Empire.

Disclaimer

Even though the author and publisher have made every effort to make sure the content in this book is current at the time of printing, and even though this publication is meant to give accurate information about the topic it covers, the author and publisher disclaim any liability for any kind of loss, impairment caused by oversight or mistakes whether due to default, mishap, or any other cause.

Contents

Dedication v
Disclaimer vii
Narcissism Rising! The Final World Empire xiii

1 The Man of Lawlessness 1
2 USA Rise to Superpower 6
3 The World is Getting Ready 10
4 Globalism and the Tower of Babel 13
5 The Weather, Environment, and Wealth 17
6 America is No Longer a Christian Nation 23
7 A Digital Currency & Digital ID 26
8 Narcissism Rising 28
9 Deception, Despair, Fear & Hope In Christ 34
10 Apostasy, Changing Rules & Laws 37
11 Ten Kings, The Beast, Rapture 40
12 The Fall of Rome & End of Civilization 43
13 Faithfully Dedicated 47
14 You Will Own Nothing and be Happy. 50

15 Narcissists are Spiritually Dark 56

16 The Final World Empire & Church Age Ends 59

17 Reprobates & Normalcy Rejected 62

18 A Dark Regime 66

19 The Seven Seals Open 70

20 Seventh Seal: 144,000 Jewish Evangelists Sealed & Trumpet Judgments. 88

21 The Antichrist & Mid-Tribulation 93

22 Seven Vials" Poured Upon Earth 98

23 Mystery Babylon 102

24 A World View, Narcissism 106

25 A Society Based on Lies 109

26 The Marriage Supper & Second Coming 114

27 More Things That Will Take Place 118

28 The Great Invasion 123

29 Global Governance Advancing & Famine 125

30 Corrupt Narcissistic Rulers 130

31 The Ideology of The Final World Empire 133

32 One Health Agenda 136

33 One World Food-Production 142

34 A Depraved Narcissistic Mindset 147

35 America's Freedom's Fall 151

36 Revived Sodom 154

37	Concerning Aspects of the Final World Empire	157
38	A Rogue Regime	161
39	They are Speeding Up Their Global Efforts	165
40	A Spiritual Battle	168
41	Everything Falling into Place	171
42	The Downward Spiral Acceleration	175
43	Did You Ever Expect It to Happen In Your Lifetime	178
44	Signs & Warnings	181
45	Too Late for America	185
46	The UN's New Plan	189
47	CBDCs (Central Bank Digital Chip)	193
48	Signs in the Heavens	195
49	The Millennial Reign of Jesus Christ	199
50	Be Ready	203
51	Epilogue – July 2023	206

About The Author 209

Narcissism Rising! The Final World Empire

Introduction

The Book of Daniel and Revelation are two Prophetic books that adequately describe specific events; political, economic, and spiritual changes drastically in the world's societies as cultures crumble, the destruction of morals and traditions, lawlessness increases, and right is wrong. Wrong is correct, and "Truth" no longer matters.

We slowly watch the fabric of our society peeling away and becoming unrecognizable. These events and many more are happening now on the world stage, as predicted long ago. Those who have studied the ancient writings in the Prophetic Books can understand what is happening in our World. Others do not know what to expect and will be part of the "sheeple" that wander around in despair and uncertainty.

End times abound! The signs are everywhere, and watching those events predicted is a "warning" to prepare. As these events pass, more will increase in intensity and culminate. When this happens, 'The Final World Empire' will come to fruition, and a ruthless tyrant will head it and control every human being on earth, as the scriptures tell us.

At the same time, we are witnessing those events come to pass; we see something else rising in the minds of humanity today. Narcissism is increasing in our culture like never before. According to the

Prophetic texts, evil men and seducers worsen as time passes, bringing us closer to that Final World Empire.

It is not surprising, but everywhere you look, it is noticeable that narcissists are running this world system. Many social media send out content that is "masked" as the correct information, and some media do not report accurate information. Some corporations, banking, medical, education, sports, Hollywood, political leaders, and church leaders all show signs of Narcissism.

As we approach the culmination of everything foretold to us in the ancient texts about the soon-to-be-coming Final World Empire, it will put us on a path of devastating climactic events never before seen in the history of this present world. We are already seeing some of this coming to pass.

The ruthless world leader will soon appear on the world stage, making Adolf Hitler look like a choir boy, and the rules and laws he put into place will be for complete control of all of humanity. This coming world dictator will be a full-blown Malignant Narcissist.

The world stage is already halfway set for the ushering in of the Narcissistic World leader known to many as the Anti-Christ or Beast of Revelation. As you read, his supporters are preparing the way for his debut even now. They are those that have the anti-christ spirit and like-mindedness of the Beast they follow. They have a Narcissistic nature as their leader, the lawless one.

This book is a culmination of Prophetic Events that have come to pass and are soon to be, as predicted, that will usher in the Final World Empire for those who have eyes to see and ears to hear. The time is late; prepare!

1

The Man of Lawlessness

The Apostle Paul describes the soon-to-be-leader of the Final World Empire as "The Man of Lawlessness." He will oppose all religions, including Judeo-Christian beliefs.

He will sit in the newly rebuilt temple in Jerusalem, claiming to be God. For such a person to proclaim to the World that he is God, he must be a distinctive type of person; and has such an exaggerated view of himself; he expects all the World to worship and adore him as God. Individuals that refuse to adhere to such demands will face torture. Certainly, someone with this mannerism is a malignant narcissist. In addition to his claims to be God, he will dominate the globe for three and one-half years, and at the helm of an unseen military force, the entire World will be under his control.

In the Book of Daniel, "The Man of Lawlessness" is used similarly to what the Apostle Paul described. Both prophets portray him as having a "haughty" mouth speaking great things and blasphemies toward the Almighty as he oppresses God's people. He also changes God and nature's "rules and laws" as he chooses.

This world leader feels entitled to do whatever he desires. His blasphemous negligence for respect of God and His rules, as well as God's people, and sinful condemnation of overstepping those rules and laws put in place by the "Highest" is meaningless to him.

He will cause all earth dwellers to pledge allegiance to him and his regime and to take his mark on their forehead or right arm. Without his mark, you will not be able to buy or sell. Those who refuse to obey this monster will be subject to legislation requiring immediate torture and execution.

This psychopathic narcissist world dictator will employ the false prophet who works for him so that his narcissistic cult's oppressive regulations are law. As the ancient texts predict, it is safe to say that this global world leader will show no mercy to those who refuse to follow him. Millions will die because they refuse to bow to this evil tyrant, the Anti-Christ or Beast of Revelation.

We can detect that this type of individual's personality is nothing short of a psychopath, consumed with Narcissistic traits and possessed by Satan. He has grandiosity and superior nature, a desire to control humanity with his global authority. Envy, hypersensitive to rejection, inability to feel compassion, and depravity are all characteristics of his temperament. It is the personality of the soon-to-be leader of the Final World Empire, and his supporters and followers are already preparing the way for him to appear on the world stage.

It is hard to imagine how such a diverse array of human characteristics may survive the personality of a single individual. A craving for domination over all humanity, boastfulness, evil, intolerance to offense, and especially to such an extreme degree of egomania. Brilliance and exceptionalism this tyrant will acquire.

All these characteristics in a single person are not coincidental. Several professionals in the medical field have studied dictators and tyrants, and they have observed certain traits in their personalities and character.

The leader of the Final World Empire (Antichrist) is an evil individual, and the scriptures tell us Satan will empower him. A predominant trait of such a person is scapegoating, and he will focus his attention on people who follow the Judeo-Christian belief. His scapegoating tactics will convince a portion of the World that believers are enemies of the World. Sadly, many will believe his habitual lies. We are already seeing the hatred of believers rising.

When the Beast comes on the world stage, he will come at a time when the whole World is in turmoil, and he will have all the solutions to the problems in the World. He will appear as the Savior of humanity. This individual is called the Beast in ancient texts for a reason. He is a Beast, a monster in disguise. He wears a "mask" to deceive the World; as all Narcissists hide their true motives, so will the Beast.

He will have a Seven Year covenant drawn up and signed with many offering Peace to Israel. It is described in the scriptures as the Tribulation or the Time of Jacobs's Trouble. Midway through seven years, his "mask" comes off, revealing his true nature. Satan will then possess him in his madness and insanity. This evil will kill millions, and the Jewish people will suffer at his hands immensely. He will stop the Jews from sacrificing in the newly built temple, something he promised them at the beginning of signing the seven-year covenant. All the Jewish people will then understand he is an imposter and not someone who is there to bring peace and help them in the land and from their enemies.

The Beast world leader believes himself to be blameless and blames everyone who disagrees with his policies and will execute many. He requires complete devotion from all earth dwellers, and his perception of himself is magnificent and excellent.

The Beast is a malignant narcissist who is the worst form of Narcissism. It is because he has a defect in his soul as he is unwilling to submit his will to God, and he offers his choice to the enemy of his soul, Satan.

Evil people are willing to gravitate toward evil to get their way, and they ignore all guilt. The malignant world leader has a remarkable power behind him and feels no remorse or compassion for those opposing him. The energy he acquires is from insolent pride, the root cause of all narcissists. This great pride and arrogance are displayed for one reason, to control all humanity.

The World Leader's desire for control of the globe results from a "reprobate" mind. He feels no guilt, shame, or remorse for his ruthless actions and no regard for human life. It is a total rebellion against the most "High." He proclaims himself God.

You may question how malignant narcissists may attain positions of global leadership. It is not uncommon for individuals with narcissistic personalities to hold positions of authority. In the past, politicians have wrestled with Narcissism and have had successful careers.

Some of those in authority who displayed narcissist traits are Starlin, Mao Tso-tung, and others. They were known to acquire such characteristics and were successful in their careers. The malignant leader, Adolf Hitler, topped the list of all such leaders.

In extreme cases of malignant Narcissism, those are people who have managed to elevate themselves to positions of power but who have a history of succumbing to brutalities and authoritarian regimes as a result of their positive advantages.

Throughout its history, western democracy has sometimes displayed mannerisms that have made it possible for the most reprehensible politicians to reign in leadership roles, including those who are tyrants for the sake of power and wealth.

The main point is to be aware of world leaders who have the solutions to all the World's problems when chaos arises. These leaders appear to be the redeemers in a world out of control.

The Hope for a political messiah in the United States and worldwide remains high in this era, as we see Chaos, Violence, Lawlessness, and Terror everywhere. The news media updates "hourly" tragic events that are happening on a global scale.

Our World is turned upside down as we no longer recognize the normalcy of living in a peaceful world. The ancient texts predicted long ago all such events we are witnessing daily, and situations would continue to grow worse on a global scale.

We are halfway through the construction process for the completion of ushering in a utopia that global world leaders have decided for us by their 2030 Agenda. The malignant Narcissist's world leader is waiting in the shadows to come onto the World's center stage and lead humanity in a New World.

We will explore all events that will put humanity on a path leading to the ultimate Final World Empire.

2

USA Rise to Superpower

Before World War 1, Germany, France, Great Britain, and Italy were the leading suppliers of goods and services worldwide. The Great War destroyed almost all the nations in Europe, and even though France and Great Britain were superpowers, the conflict war caused those countries to experience bankrupt conditions. Much of their manufacturing business came to a halt as companies shut down.

The globalist devised a plan to make America the new superpower because the country's geographic location was far from the war zone. As European manufacturing facilities closed, counterparts opened in the United States. They ramped up manufacturing and began supplying enormous quantities to Europe and other regions worldwide. It resulted in large amounts of money being lent to those countries at extremely high-interest rates.

The increase in production in the United States during the war is mainly responsible for America's rise as the World's superpower. Since the conclusion of World War 11, America has been a pivotal actor in the global system, which has resulted in the creation of numerous new international organizations, including the Worldwide Monetary Fund, the United Nations, the World Economic Forum, and NATO.

Multilateral accords on commerce, environment, global stability, and nuclear disarmament have all been significantly aided by U.S. engagement.

Since the 1950's politicians and world leaders are diligently moving forward to establish a one-world government, the Final World Empire. It has become more of a concern because numerous countries ceded their sovereignty to the United Nations, Bosnia, Somalia, and Kuwait are just a few of those countries.

In addition, International accords like NAFTA and GATT are two of the most significant trade agreements in recent history; they provided countries a voice in regulating trade and labor practices beyond the scope of the wars.

The Dominance of America is Fading

The global political system is experiencing an explosive transformation that will give rise to an incredibly different design in the future. America is slowly losing the superpower status we once knew.

Since no global superpower has a unifying force, the door is open for a charismatic leader to emerge from the population and integrate the globe under his Final World Empire.

Circumstances, such as the state of the economy around the World, will bring about poverty to most of the globe, and the accumulation of riches will fall into the hands of a selected few individuals at the expense of the vast majority of the World's people.

Those with their hands on the wealth will rule the World's economies and governments. To minimize revenues, significant corporations will merge. It has led to the rise of a global corporate elite with no obligation to any country or state and whose only concern is making money for themselves and shareholders. Ordinary people of the World will be reduced to peasants, while corporate heads will act more like Kings to safeguard their firm's wealth. Those in control will support and usher in the international tyrant, the world dictator.

The Decline of America

America is in decline, as factual reports are revealing this daily:

- The Supply Chain is in severe disruption.
- Homelessness and national debt are out of control.
- The nation's infrastructure, including its ports and highways, is dismal.
- Our energy stockpile is rapidly dwindling.
- The train systems are going off the rails across the country.
- Our open borders have allowed criminals, narcotics, and terrorists to flood the land.
- Many people die from fentanyl overdose every year.
- The United States is experiencing an uptick in violent crime and retail theft rates.
- The concept of gender identity is murky among young people in America.
- The cost of food and other necessities is rapidly increasing.
- Fires are destroying egg farms across the country.
- Animals are killed, fish are poisoned, and people are sick because of the derailment in Ohio several months ago that spreads toxic air overhead.
- The middle class is collapsing under massive inflation and much more.

Bureaucrats are creating laws and policies about the weather, affecting everyone's quality of life. We will eat bugs and worms, walk to work, and have less energy. Only the elite prosper.

Everyone on the planet will practice the global religion and those that reject it are considered enemies of the public good. They will be subjected to coercive reeducation and made to comply against their will.

Many world leaders, legislators, business moguls, academia, celebrities, and preachers are all global religion proponents.

Innumerable officials have openly proclaimed the transformation of the United States of America, and at this point, the change is nearly finished.

3

The World is Getting Ready

Some people on Earth know the World is in turmoil, and a part of the population is getting ready for fear of what they see coming. They are stockpiling food, medicines, and the bare essentials for everyday life.

For fear of nuclear war and other impending disasters, many feel the mountains are the safest place to be, and some people are even buying abandoned missile silos, turning them into lodging areas in case something dreadful happens.

After considering such terrifying scenarios, the rest of the population likely goes on to live their lives as usual.

Someone else is getting ready, and he is moving at a frantic pace throughout the process. Satan is busy doing what he does best.

We can see the results of his action by paying attention to current events. He knows his time is short, so we see an increase in his work.

Satan is influencing his malignant narcissist followers from all walks of life—the economy, entertainment, science, government, academia, churches, and more.

Just as the prophet Daniel wrote in his prophetic book about government, the technologies are shaping up for the coming "mark" of the Beast system (666) of Revelation 13. Some public schools and universities are pushing anti-God ideologies in academia. Science advances rapidly to bring humanity under a total surveillance system that will aid Satan's "Man of Lawlessness," the leader of the Final World Empire, to control the World's population.

By watching events unfolding in the World, it appears humanity is adapted to the Worship of a sinister entity, the devil. The Super Bowl halftime show and Grammy's of 2023 displayed nothing short of prayers and Worship of the demonic figure as people cheered and applauded.

Certain officials met to discuss 'the weather" on Mount Sinai in Egypt, where God handed Moses the Ten Commandments in stone. Upon their descent from the mountain, they had their Religion as well written, the Ten Weather Commandments. It was nothing short of "blasphemy" and "mockery" to God.

What is happening to young children in this era is incomprehensible. As the scriptures tell the story about Lot's Day, Sodom, and Gomorrah, it is worse in our Day.

The ancient text tells us evil men and seducers will worsen. The preparation by a sinister entity is getting the World ready for a wicked, malignant narcissist leader to come on the world stage, known as the dictator of the Final World Empire, the AntiChrist.

It is almost impossible for those unfamiliar with Bible Prophecy to understand what unfolds as we watch the "signs of the times."

The world stage is set, and most of humanity will welcome, with open arms, the Narcissist's world leader and gladly take his "mark" on their right hand or forehead as they pledge allegiance to the Beast and his Narcissistic Cult.

Satan is preparing to fight against all during the Tribulation Period. He has progressed in all his strategies thus far. He will continue in intensity as his destruction pushes humanity to the brink of despair and hopelessness as they watch events unfold, drawing closer to that Final World Empire.

4

Globalism and the Tower of Babel

Globalists have transformed the story of the Tower of Babel found in the Bible into an ideology. According to prophetic writings, everyone living during that time was fluent in one language. In their arrogance and foolishness, they erected a great tower to try and reach God and Heaven.

Because God was so angry with what they did, He cut off their ability to speak to one another, and they were spread out around the Earth. God was humiliated by humanity's collective defiance of Him.

Today's Tower of Babel

According to antiquity, the incentives behind constructing the Tower of Babel are startlingly akin to those fueling globalism today. Wealthy individuals no longer feel responsible to God for their actions and behavior because of the Babel philosophy developed around them. They think they can create a "Utopia" and open Heaven's gates, becoming gods.

Wealthy bureaucrats have three things in mind, power, greed, and wealth.

The concept that globalists exist was nothing more than a wild conspiracy theory at one time. Furthermore, the objective of a cashless society and a global government was held in the tightest secrecy and only mentioned in mainstream conversation. Those that tried to tell the public were called crazy.

I recall scoffing and mockery myself when trying to reason with others about such information. Elected officials, heads of state, the WEF, the United Nations, the Media, and others currently support it.

The notion that these instances are examples of "conspiracy theory is no longer credible in modern times. The people who used smear campaigns and mocked the "truth tellers" now look ignorant, given that globalists are bombarding the mainstream with this knowledge.

Decades of deception and misinformation have forced people into accepting a global monetary system and one-world government. If the broader public is misled into buying an ideology, that idea is essentially defective.

Bureaucrats may declare their objective for globalization to the public, but are they also informing the critical implications resulting from their agenda?

Elites Perspective:

- Globalists want to dominate and govern every aspect of culture and shape humanity according to the mold they envision.
- They want to live without cash because all transactions, including investments and purchases, can be monitored. They can limit all resources, turning the system into the parent figure. You are entirely unable to manage your financial concerns.
- Bureaucrats despise sovereignty and borders of nations. They wish to rule as monarchs over a global empire.

- They prefer an unaccountable monopoly-style government run behind closed doors by an unchecked elite.
- To coerce the public into supporting global authority, "sustainability" has replaced the more familiar term "environmentalism." They say climate and the environment justify curbing specific foods, the size of families, and the amount of power supply individuals use.
- Another topic of conversation among the privileged is pollution. It discusses that humanity represents a substantial risk to the environment. To convince people to surrender to mother earth by making them believe they pose a significant danger to the planet.
- They identify as "guardians" of the Earth and self-identify in that capacity.
- The elite's ideological base is eugenics, and they believe in biological management and observation. Those deemed inappropriate will face severe sanctions.

The Eugenics movement in the United States started at the beginning of the century thanks to the Rockerfella Foundation. At the World's Fair, a celebration was held in its honor. The government of the state of California passed eugenics laws, which resulted in the forcible sterilization of thousands of people. Germany adopted the method in the 1930s when it was known for its cruelty.

The ruling class is under the notion that only four percent of the population possesses the necessary genetic makeup to hold positions of power. They are under the impression that they are a component of that four percent.

Eugenics was unpopular after WW11. This time, the movement is returning under the banner of "the Weather" and the need to save the planet.

The governing class under the Final World Empire will determine who survives, dies, and is fit to be born. Eugenics will be the technology of population structure in the future.

It's important to remember that the argument about the four percent leadership originally appeared in the periodicals published by the ruling class. The percentage of people with underlining malignant Narcissism is four percent. Can this be just a happy accident?

Malignant narcissists are psychopaths who lack empathy and are self-absorbed. They have vivid imaginations and believe themselves to be Kings among humanity. They regard the regular people beneath them and live to amuse themselves and for easing their elevation to godhead.

Habitual lying is a narcissist's trait used in many narratives to fit the agenda. The conversation is always one-sided and never allows a different viewpoint from their own. They crave power more than anything else, particularly the ability to rule over humanity and thrive on the goods the average person supplies.

The worldwide Cultic Religion to which the privileged owe their power promotes moral relativism, self-worship, and using any means required to achieve godhead. It fits internationalism perfectly.

As a result of the cooperation between the United Nations and Lucis Trust, also known as" Lucifer Publishing Company," its organization is the only ideological institution the global conglomerate sponsors. Its unique library is located within the United Nations headquarters.

The new modern-day "Tower of Babel" is being constructed. The signs are everywhere, showing that the construction movement is nearing completion. All will hail the Narcissistic dictator of the Final World Empire once he comes on the world stage.

5

The Weather, Environment, and Wealth

America has led the World in economics, freedoms, and liberties, but other individuals want to destroy it and are no longer happy with the success the country experienced. The trends set here in this country branch out into other nations, and if America falls, so goes the World.

The equal distribution of wealth is critical for both Communism and Socialism. Such people defend the rights of some groups of people while denying such rights to others and robbing them (Distribution of Wealth). The objective is convincing the victim that the perpetrators have their best interests in mind.

The Imperialist ambition to construct their Global Government, New World Order, or Great Reset by 2030 or sooner is progressing quickly. It is the "Final World Empire" spoken of by Daniel the prophet.

The Weather

They are marketing the "fear" tactic to the public that the planet will be destroyed due to human activity. Taxation will be utilized to protect the globe from the weather, and using only electric power will clean up the World, and the planet will be freed.

The best source of electricity generation in the future will be wind turbines, as officials jet around the World in luxury, and wind turbines, batteries, and charging stations have already begun to be manufactured by several companies.

These endeavors are made possible through the transfer of wealth, funded by taxes, government contracts, and backroom negotiations.

Exploiting slave labor in some countries is used to extract the hazardous components of batteries. At the same time, enterprises plunder natural resources at the expense of lives and the environment.

A classic example is California; the state advocated for electric cars but could not meet the primary energy demand. It led to repeated brownouts in the sweltering heat during the summer months and forced residents to stop charging their vehicles.

According to some reports, the presence of windmills in the waters off the coast of New Jersey is devastatingly impacting the ecosystem, leading to the deaths of many whales, fish, and birds.

The new forms of environmental terrorism and modern-day slavery are caused by organizations that inspire the public with empty ecological slogans. They are pocketing the money and ignoring the victims, the people.

Narcissism is Rising! Self-Entitlement is a trait of Narcissistic individuals, they take from others, and entitlement allows them to do so without feeling it is wrong.

Components of World Government Forming

As mentioned previously about the Tribulation and the Beast leader,

According to ancient texts (some Old Testament), the last seven years of gentile world domination will be what the Bible calls The Tribulation, during the "Final World Empire."

The ruling class striving to usher in global governance believes it will be a "New Era" they have always envisioned. Such individuals are not aware that they are indeed fulfilling biblical prophecy.

The organizers and governing class are instrumental in transforming our current world system into a New World System and will have their World Government, but it will only be for a short time, the prophecies tell us.

To better understand, let us look back into the ancient texts on the subject matter:

The beginning of the gentile world power started long ago when King Nebuchadnezzar was head over the Medo-Persian Empire. Daniel was one of the many Jewish youths taken captive in Babylon in the first siege under King Nebuchadnezzar.

Daniel exceeded in wisdom and ultimately rose to become among the three highest officers in the Medo-Persian Empire. He wrote historical records in Babylon, including "The Book of Daniel." It is a book in the Bible about Kings and Kingdoms, of thrones and dominations.

While including some ancient records, it incorporates prophecies of the progression of nations and territories in the "Time of Gentile World Power." It sums up the End of the Gentile World domain.

The "Book" depicts events prophesied to occur during this age and culminate in the devastating End of the "Gentile World Order" at the Return of Jesus, Messiah, who will bring it all to an End.

Daniel writes about events of great persecution during "The Final

World Empire" toward Christians and the Jewish people and the ultimate blasphemies toward those people and God by the Malignant Narcissist's World leader, the Antichrist.

Pre-Tribulation Gateway

It has been noticeable and evident the surge of depravity that has infiltrated our existence in the last couple of years. Nothing resembles normality to the extent that it did just a few years ago.

There is undeniably an abnormal atmosphere surrounding our lives today that was not present in the past, and it is not emanating from the light but darkness. I feel prompted to acknowledge by the Holy Spirit that it is a reality; an assault on humanity is occurring.

I will refer to the infiltration of the abnormal atmosphere as coming from "Pre-Tribulation Gateways. Such activity appears to be infiltrating, if not dominating, our existence. Because the demonic activity is so strong, a "Pre-Tribulation" assault is taking place in our time before the Lord calls His faithful followers' home in the Rapture.

Everything is leading up to the Antichrist reign of terror Jesus foretold to be the darkest time in the history of humanity. As the faithful are taken off the planet, and the (Daniel 9) covenant is signed with many, Satan is preparing the stage for his man of Lawlessness to reign as King in the Final World Empire.

In the United States, the planning started in earnest shortly after the turn of the twentieth century. It picked up speed, and we are now operating at maximum capacity.

When the courts began removing God from their decision-making, the assault began. The wickedness forced upon the children is possibly the essential evidence of what is flooding through the Pre-tribulation gateways.

It is an intense version of depravity, and even parents appear to have lost any moral resistance they may have had against the destructive toxins of Satan, humanity's worst enemy.

Top officials in the land's stance on children are irrefutable evidence that the United States has reached the depraved mindset of Romans 1:28.

Children need to be protected. Can there be any mistake that the gateways of the Pre-Tribulation era are wide open with this kind of deprivation visited upon America's youth?

Components Leading to World Government

The Final World Empire will be commanded by the Narcissistic dictator, Beast of Revelation 13, and his inner circle, with the "lower class" serving them. The "lower class" cannot exceed 500 million, so a population decline exists.

The evidence-based facts of the pandemic have been made public. Therefore, they had the plan to achieve the purpose of eliminating more of the "lower class."

Georgia Guidestones

On the strange Georgia Guidestones are ten "commandments" for a New Era of Reason. The first of the ten commandments is, "Keep the human population below 500 million and In Harmony With Nature." It would necessitate eradicating five-sixths of the globe's population, which is "half of humanity."

Event 201

John Hopkins Health and Security sponsored **"Event 201,"** a pandemic tabletop exercise in collaboration with the World Health Organization and the Bill & Milinda Gates Foundation.

The Simulated Event

The scenario recreated an outbreak of a previously unknown zoonotic coronavirus that spread from bats to pigs to people and, ultimately, rapidly distributed from person to person, resulting in a devasting pandemic.

The infectious agent and the symptoms it causes are based heavily on SARS but are more contagious among residents when only moderate signs appear. There is no chance for a vaccine to be available within the first year.

The combined instances climb enormously, increasing every week, because the whole human race is vulnerable in the early months of the outbreak. The economic and social repercussions become more severe, and illnesses and deaths rise.

Until an effective vaccine or 80-90% of the World's population has been affected, the pandemic will continue to rise.

Only a few weeks after the conclusion of Event 201, Covid 19 got underway. A severe thought to question?

The Continuation of Event 201

In addition to the first simulated event, they are followed by the "real" pandemic; another devastating infectious pandemic exercise was created on October 23, 2022. Bill & Melinda Gates Foundation, John Hopkins Center for Health Security, and the World Health Organization are the same organizations.

It acted as a reproduction of several meetings held by the World Health Organization Emergency Health Advisory Board to discuss a manufactured pandemic that would occur shortly.

Delegates contended how to respond to an infectious illness that spreads swiftly and becomes a pandemic with a high death rate, worse than covid 19, and primarily affects children and adolescents.

Are the Georgia Guidestones erected as a primary purpose to give us warning of what to expect?

6

America is No Longer a Christian Nation

America was once a Christian country but is now a post-Christian nation. This country and other Western nations are enforcing a New Established Religion upon everyone.

Every substantial part of society, including the media, big tech, government, entertainment, academia, corporations, and business, are all doing their part to promote "Wokeism" upon the planet.

Powerful dictatorial unbelievers enforce this New International movement.

God is not part of this powerful movement, and He is allowing it to occur, just as predicted in Romans 1:28.

The influential and authoritarian atheists enforce this new movement.

They are laying the theological and governmental stage for the Antichrist and False Prophet, who will control the planet during the

Final World Empire. These two men are the most influential figures on the earth.

Fourteen-Year Transition Period

The World is transitioning from more than 190 sovereign nations to one global government over 14 years (2016-2030).

More than halfway through that transformation phase, history is inexorably advancing toward a totalitarian Final World Empire dominated by Narcissistic officials.

Their New International Religion

About the enforcement of this new movement in the country. Six kids from a California high school performed in drag as part of a school-sponsored drag queen concert.

Gender-confused drag queens wore wigs and dresses and danced on the gym floor as they removed their clothing. Attendance was mandatory for all students as drag queens preached their agenda.

In response to the objections, school administrators stated that the dragqueen presentation fully conforms with student standards of conduct and existing procedures for on-campus events.

The West Spreading Their New Movement

Other accounts indicate that the President of Uganda slammed the Western nations for attempting to enforce their New movement on his country.

The U.S. Border

U.S. Border Patrol Chief informed the U.S. Homeland Security Committee that it is not in operational control of the border.

If the border is not secure, someone is deceiving the American people.

A Falling Away in the Church

Jesus and the Prophets often called Hell a real place when preaching to the people. However, the Vatican leader tells us that Hell is not a real place and that no person is in a place called Hell.

Persecution of Christians

The United Kingdom Parliament voted to criminalize prayer, even silent prayer, near an abortion center.

During the Tribulation, in the Final World Empire, individuals who become believers in Jesus Christ will be forbidden to pray to God but forced to pray to a monument of the Antichrist. Multitudes will be killed because they refuse to bow down to the memorial. All Bibles will be banned, and those caught with one will be considered committing "hate crimes" for the common good of society. Re-Education camps are where they will be sent; if they don't renounce their faith, they will be martyred.

The ancient texts tell us that the Narcissistic World Leader will change "rules & laws."

How quickly do we see "laws & rules" already changing in this era? Things not recognizable just five years ago are now at center stage.

Christians are put on the terrorist watch list, and it will not be long before they must meet secretly for prayer and Worship for fear of being caught.

The scriptures have much to say in the Book of Daniel and Revelation about the great persecution believers in God suffered during the Final World Empire.

7

A Digital Currency & Digital ID

A digital I.D. will be issued to all humanity to use the forthcoming digital currency. It may be just a matter of a few months before a digital currency is introduced; However, it will take time to enroll financial institutions and businesses, and the ability to track purchases and sales only needs to be operational by the middle of the Tribulation Period, lasting three and one-half years after the Final World Empire.

The transformation of America into a New World System is undeniably taking place, yet most people are unaware of what is at stake. With churches on every corner, at one time, people can learn the Truth at once in America.

Sadly, the days of learning the "truth" of God and His desire for humanity have ended. "Truth" no longer exists, at least in America's churches, and it is replaced with "vanity," teaching a "worldly view" of the biblical doctrine Christ and His apostles set forth.

Nothing is left when God is outlawed in society, but an empty void and the people perish.

As the Book of Ecclesiastes tells us:

"To everything, there is a season and a time to every purpose under the Heaven."

As we watch the "Old America" transform into the New World System they are creating, it is important to remember; we are witnessing prophecy unfold just as Jesus pronounced it would take place in this time frame.

The Antichrist spirit works in the hearts and minds of all his followers, doing what they are called to do to prepare the way for him and his associate, the false prophet.

Nothing is unnoticed by the God of the Christians and Jewish people, and he allows everything to happen so that evil will destroy itself in the End. All followers of the Highest God of the Universe will possess the "Real and Final Kingdom" when Jesus restores the Earth after the Tribulation, and we live and reign with Him for a thousand years in the Millennial Kingdom.

The components of the 'Final World Empire' are everywhere; those that don't notice changes going on either don't want to see or favor a New system being constructed.

Time is at hand, as we are approaching the Midnight hour!

8

Narcissism Rising

It is good and evil in the World, and God has created a consciousness in every human being to choose between that good and evil.

A selfish individual always gravitates toward the bad, and it is because they have no moral compass to guide them. They do not believe in objective Truth; only their truth reality matters.

Narcissism has existed since almost the beginning of time, and there are many forms. Some are more severe forms than others.

Many hardcore narcissists have become what the term implies as malignant narcissists. They are beyond receiving any "factual information." They live in an alternative universe and have a warped mindset.

The Bible describes their warped thinking as a "reprobate mindset" (Romans 1:28). They refused to receive the "truth," so God turned them over to a reprobate mind.

It is essential to understand that if anyone disagrees with a narcissist, they are so sensitive they take it as criticism, which is something they do not tolerate

Narcissists believe they are superior to everyone else. Their World revolves around them, and if you disagree with them, it exposes their wrong, which is unacceptable behavior.

Malignant selfish individuals do not want to share the planet with anyone who opposes their distorted belief system. They will try to convince you they are right and know better than the average person. It does not matter how much evidence you have to prove their wrongdoing, it simply will not matter, and they will steamroll right over your truthful facts.

An average person should not waste their time reasoning with selfish people in hopes they will accept your presentation of information. It is better to take the Truth, knowing they are unredeemable people.

Spiritually speaking, God can redeem anyone, but the person must first admit he is wrong. Malignant narcissists are unredeemable because they believe they are always right and never wrong; therefore, trying to prove your case of information to a Malignant Narcissist is a waste of mental energy. Your "truthfulness," as far as they are concerned, will be ignored.

Control is a primary trait of Narcissism, and some globalists are malignant narcissists who want to control everyone on Earth. They are aggressively forming their New World System according to their ideology.

Narcissistic officials use their wealth to control the World we live in, and as previously mentioned, their influence is in every aspect of society. They are sociopaths and psychopaths that organize and plan their agenda for the World as they impose their corrupt effect on the populace.

Narcissistic figureheads dictate their objective to humanity and expect complete compliance with the decisions made.

Such individuals are harmful to everyone because of their delusional and fragmented decisions.

The idea to "Transform" the World into a New System should

have been a wake-up call to many; sadly, it is ignored by most, and now we are left with a broken system and much corruption.

The point is this; Narcissistic wealthy individuals are dominating this World and restructuring it following their warped ideology.

The enemy is within the gates and has decided what we shall eat, where we will live, what and who we will worship, and so on. Once they usher in the Final World Empire, their requirements for the World's population will be dramatically contrary to our traditional way of life.

As Klaus Schwab, President of the WEF, said, we will own nothing and be happy.

Their ultimate goal in their coming New World Utopia is Transhumanism, and that is, merging humans with machines. Yuval Noah Harari, Klaus Schwab's close associate, is a strong proponent of Transhumanism.

Narcissism is Rising! All the Prophecies God gave us is to warn humanity to prepare. Be sure you are in the right standing with God. There is no other way, and Jesus is humanity's Hope.

The World is off balance, and evil individuals planned it that way.

Tribulation gateways are open and will grow wider as demonic entities flood the Earth.

I can't help but continue to focus on what they are doing to the children. Children sit before drag queens and watch them take their clothes off. It is hard to write about because I have searched for the right words to put in print.

Hell is empty, and the demons are here and victimizing the children. I never thought I would see parents of young children allow them to participate by being the drag queens' audience and watching them expose themselves to the children.

Some high officials tell us it's shameful and sinful not to allow seven-year-old children to get mutilated and put on puberty blockers.

If eighteen-year-olds choose to get their body parts mutilated, no one is telling them they cannot. However, young children being exploited in such a way is unacceptable.

We are at war, and it is a spiritual war for Civilization. The demonic realm influences narcissists' delusional mindset, and they are trying to destroy humanity, and children are the targets.

The ancient texts tell us that they sacrificed their children to idols. (Ezekiel 16:21). It is the same thing they do today to the children. They may not be blood sacrifices at this time; however, the horrors of the Tribulation period during the Final World Empire will be graphic.

We have witnessed unprecedented Lawlessness in just the past few years. Crime is rampant, evil has no restraints and is becoming increasingly worse as depravity flourishes and goodness and Truth are banished.

I don't have to go far in my community to witness the increase in abnormal behavior in some individuals. Watching daily news has reached its proportion on Lawlessness as sinister events in all areas of society rise.

We are witnessing the Earth's populations explode in engrossed Narcissistic activity, known as sin. If God is ignored and not present in people's lives, we are left empty, and that is when Satan moves in to fill that empty void in people.

Jesus warned us that at the close of time, conditions on Earth would be just as in the days of Noah and Lot.

People did their everyday business until the flood came, and Noah and his family entered the ark. The people ignored the warnings when Noah told them what would occur, and instead, they mocked and scoffed. The very Day Noah and his family entered the ark, the rains began, and God shut the door to the ark.

It is no different today; people are too busy and don't have time to consider the cost; sadly, it will be too late, just as Jesus predicted.

The same situation occurred during Lot's Day. The people were engrossed in wickedness, and Lot was the only righteous person, and his family and God spared them. The Day he and his family left the city as the angel instructed them to, fire and brimstone rained down on the cities of Sodom and Gomorrah.

Evil was so rampant during Noah's and Lot's days that God had to destroy everyone except two righteous families.

The point is this; If Jesus specifically names Noah and Lot and compares our generation to that timeframe, don't you think it is essential to heed the warning?

Conditions in our era are precisely like the days of Noah and Lot, if not worse.

Narcissism is Rising! Insanity abounds. Humanity is on a path to destruction, just as in the Days of Noah and Lot.

Malignant narcissistic sociopaths have brought humanity into the dark realm, leading the World's population over the cliff into the abyss.

Following the trends of the times set forth by malignant narcissists, they have set a precedent by conditioning people to include children in certain lifestyles that would be a prison sentence to anyone who did such things just a few years back.

Following the trends of today by evil perpetrators, in the end, will cause you to lose your soul.

It is hard to stand alone, especially against a "Cult" of influential individuals, but following such trends they have set for you is Anti-God.

Everything comes down to decision-making based on your values, character, and worldview.

Stand against the demonic that have conditioned society into fragmented and delusional thinking.

We only have one chance at getting right with God on this side of the grave, and it will bc too late any other way.

Narcissism is Rising! And increasing in speed to engulf all

humanity as it stretches its evil claws toward all people, especially the children who need to be protected from insanity.

9

Deception, Despair, Fear & Hope In Christ

We live in a culture of despair, falsehood, and fear.

Unfortunately, many of the higher class are indoctrinated into a culture of falsehood that is skilled intentionally by those committed to outside forces.

Not all (but many) are deceived in the modern-day "educational" system, and they have become agents of the wrong side.

Most of that group are simple "grooming" agents to ensure the deception promoted by an evil entity is recognized as "truth," and such lies bring despair.

They have rejected the Truth God provides; as a result, they do not take His warnings of impending disasters seriously, both here and for eternity.

"Woe" to those that call good evil and evil good. (Isaiah 5:20-21).

When God uses the word "Woe," the results will terrify that person.

Preserving Satan does not exist is one of the tools they use to deceive. However, that perception is far from the Truth.

The ancient texts tell us perfectly that there is a real enemy of our soul called Satan, who is out to destroy humanity and take as many people to Hell as he can.

Despite God's Word on the Truth of such an entity and his intentions toward humanity, some worship the great deceiver, the father of lies.

God has given His promise of Salvation through His Son, Jesus Christ, to all who resist the evil tyrant, Satan, and because of God's promises to all who submit to Christ, Satan is on the rampage to defeat the "Highest" and all who follow Him.

There is no limit to the Depravity and Hate of such an evil entity that he will provoke humanity into.

In attempting to bombard and overwhelm people with information to divert their attention away from the natural source of Hope, the collaborators of the Final World Empire have utilized their strategies to create fear and despair in the World.

In the grand scheme of things, there is no way to evade the influence of such a hostile force or escape the snares it sets for humanity in every sphere of their daily lives.

When things take a turn for the more repulsive and bizarre, it appears they cannot get more revolting; things get worse. It is because evil stretches its despicable tentacles in a God-rejecting world.

Fear, Deception, and Despair loom over the World like a thick fog, creating the erroneous impression that there is no Hope.

The primary purpose of the upholders of the Final World Empire is to instill such global despair that they can persuade people they alone have the solutions to the Earth's problems, leading people away from the genuine source of Hope.

Everyone is a target of the godless world system, prioritizing spreading deceit, fear, and hopelessness.

No government, organizations, or officials have all the answers to the World's problems.

Our "hope" is in the God of the Bible and His Son, Jesus Christ, and that Hope is what the AntiGod supporters of the Final World Empire are trying to exterminate.

Without that Hope, all is lost; and it is why we must contend for the faith, as the Apostle Jude tells us. (Jude 1:3)

Their goal in the Final World Empire is to have a one-world religion by uniting all world religions into one. The sermons preached in the pulpit of the Christian God will be limited, leaving out God, Jesus Christ, the Holy Spirit, Sin, Hell, and much more about the "true" doctrine of Jesus Christ in the Bible.

As mentioned earlier, Bibles will be banned and considered "hate crimes." We already witness the precedent set by those who despise us for our faith.

If you have faith in the divine consistent with God and His Word, the Bible teaches that people will despise us for that belief.

Hold fast to your belief in God and His Son, Jesus, and put your faith, trust, and hope in that.

Don't be swayed by the powers that be because, in the end, they will dissipate, and your reward will be abundant in eternal glory when we see our beloved Savior Jesus Christ face to face.

10

Apostasy, Changing Rules & Laws

The Lawlessness and evil dominating our World today were found in civilizations throughout history that contributed to their decline and, ultimately, destruction.

Some media, educators, and lawmakers have made God an unspeakable topic, and many churches have replaced the doctrinal purity of Christ with a watered-down version of a Christless Christianity.

Apostasy

The Bible reveals that "apostasy" will be great leading up to The Final World Empire at the End of the Age.

(2 Thessalonians 2:3) Reveals the "Great Apostasy." It is called the "Falling Away" or a rebellion from Biblical truths found in the Bible. The Apostle Paul tells us that "Apostasy" is a significant sign to watch for just before the Beast World Leader arrives.

Apostasy indicates an intentional rejection of God's revelations in a lost world.

Many people no longer accept scripture readings as "sacred texts." They have looked the other way and now prefer to hear readings and teachings on self-motivation and prosperity. They are lovers of pleasure more than lovers of God. (2 Timothy3).

Absolutes, Rules & Laws

"Professing themselves to be wise, they became fools, so God turned them over to a reprobate mind (Romans 1:22).

The above verse speaks clearly and is not hard to understand.

The spirit of this age is full-blown Narcissism! Regarding "absolutes," there is no room for the question of whether right or wrong, evil or good, and there is no in-between.

It is why many Narcissistic officials squish out "absolutes." Trying to converse with them on the subject is a hopeless cause. Their notions and policies are based on feelings and emotions and not truthful facts.

Within the past several years, we have witnessed certain officials overlooking and deliberately going against rules & laws, both spiritual as God ordained and traditional, allowing things that were once considered unseen and punishable in a court of law to be now openly accepted.

They erected the Georgia Guidestones, and on either side of the capstones is engraved, “Let these be Guidestones to an Age of Reason” in four different languages: Egyptian, Hieroglyphics, Sanskrit, and Babylonian.

Why are they written in those languages like ancient times? As mentioned earlier, they want a Final World Empire constructed as a Modern-Day Tower of Babel. They included in their text an "Age of Reason," In other words, an Age of Reason, as they are mere human beings and exclude the God of Creation, will create their Age of Reason. Not God's Age of Reason.

(Daniel 7:25) states, "He will change the Rules & Laws." The verse talks about the Antichrist.

The promoters of the Final World Empire are preparing the way for their New World System, and they are already changing the Rules & Laws to fit their "Age of Reason" in their soon-to-be New World. It will be a World Empire ruled by Narcissists and their Malignant Narcissist leader, the Beast of Revelation 13.

When the Antichrist World dictator comes onto the World stage, many of the rules and laws will have been changed, or at least set to be, and he will put the finishing touches on what he wants to add to his "Age of Reason." His changing of the Rules & Laws' origin will be literally from Hell.

Even though God will be excluded from their Age of Reason under their world system, many will follow Christ but will be martyred for their faith.

11

Ten Kings, The Beast, Rapture

According to Bible prophecy, several critical events indicate the End of the Age.

These occurrences will proceed with Daniel's 70Weeks (Tribulation) in the Final World Empire, indicating to prophetic observers the closing of this age.

The ascendance of the Seven-Headed, Ten-Horn Beast (a revised Roman Empire, the Final World Empire), the Apostle John, was shown in a vision of this Beast.

The Antichrist is the Beast ruler.

The Beast Empire will have Ten Kings (regions). The World will be divided into ten sections, with a czar (King) over each territory.

The Beast leader (Antichrist) appears after the establishment of the Ten regions, each with its monarch.

Before revealing the Antichrist, the Apostle Paul tells us the "Restrainer" will be taken out of the way; the Holy Spirit is currently "restraining" full-scale Iniquity and Lawlessness. Absolute evil on

Earth will consume Earth-dwellers, those without names written in the Book of Life in Heaven during the Final World Empire.

All committed followers of Jesus Christ that have repented sincerely of their sins and accepted Christ as Savior and Lord will be taken in what is called the "Rapture," and that is when the "restrainer" (Holy Spirit) is removed.

The Christians will be taken to Heaven to be with Jesus during the Tribulation so that God can pour His Wrath on all unbelieving earth dwellers. (John 14) tells us that Jesus is preparing a place in Heaven for His people and will soon Return for all His beloved believers who have been faithful to Him. That is what is met by the Rapture of the Church.

All those true believers who died before the Rapture will be taken first; we will meet them in the air (clouds) to be with the Savior.

(1Corinthians 15:51-52) Behold, I show you a mystery; We shall not all sleep, but be changed in a moment, in the twinkling of an eye at the last trump for the trumpet shall sound, and the dead in Christ shall be raised incorruptible, and we shall be changed.

The Beast Arises

The World leader will emerge as an influential person within the ten region confederacy, with a reputation of having a "tongue uttering great things."

Following an intense event within the ten regional territories, the malignant Narcissist's World Dictator overthrows three original Ten Kings over their domains. After these events, he emerges as the unchallenged ruler of the Beast Empire.

Once the Beast Leader solidifies his authority over the Empire, he will move to become the leader of the entire planet.

The narcissistic world leader is a great deceiver, and deception is a primary trait of Narcissism. His cunning and crafty ways deceive most of the World.

Everyone follows the World leader because he has charisma and persuasiveness, except those who understand he is a deceiver.

His ambitious initiatives to reform the Earth will usher in a time of exhilarating peace, but only for a few years.

The earth dwellers will enthusiastically support his plan to bring about changes, and the press will promote his initiatives, remarks, and activities throughout this time.

There will be an outpouring of excitement and admiration for the Narcissistic Beast dictator in all the major broadcast and cable news networks, online news, and social media.

The Beast leader is included in every news article, as reporters and the public who follow the Beast will be captivated by him, and he will be accessible around the clock.

Almost immediately, the governments of the World will make clear to the public that they accept the World Ruler over the Empire and are on board with his proposed "Great Reset" of the planet.

His magnetism charm will mesmerize the public, and Satan is his influencer, and he will capture the attention of the whole World.

Those who had put their faith and trust in Jesus at that time will be the only opposing voices to the world leader and would proclaim the Beast was a fraud, as the prophecy foretold of this time.

Individuals who listen will be told to reject the Beast's leadership at that time, and as a result, severe "hate" will be directed toward those who reject the Beast system and warn the public.

As mentioned, Christians will be executed for their faith, opposing the Beast system, and telling others the Truth about the narcissistic Beast Ruler.

12

The Fall of Rome & End of Civilization

The Final World Empire is the end of Civilization as we know it, and then a New era begins called the Millennium. It is when Jesus returns to Earth with His Bride (the Church) to set up His Kingdom for 1,000 years in Jerusalem where there is true peace & harmony. The whole World will rest as the Prophets and Jesus Himself tell us.

All sin and evil are destroyed during the Tribulation to make all things new and good for the glorious reign of Jesus the Messiah in His Kingdom on Earth.

The Beast leader and his false prophet will be thrown into the lake of fire, and all those who support the Beast when Jesus the Messiah Returns. Scripture proclaims this!

Before all this occurs, there are still more events to happen, but first, a brief look back at ancient history during the Fall of Rome:

During the second century BC, Polypus's writings described a deterioration in moral attributes that contributed to the collapse of the Roman Empire.

It appeared that the same repeated conditions harmed the Republic over time as the basic concepts, values, and customs upon which Rome was built began to deteriorate.

They were replaced by the view that life was meaningless and that immorality, banquets, greediness, and savagery were acceptable behaviors.

The Gladiator games are an excellent example of such brutality during that era.

Numerous Roman Emperors posed an additional difficulty. Caligula and Nero are excellent examples.

Nero was hostile toward the Christians then; he would hang them on a stake and set them on fire in his gardens during his banquets for entertainment.

Now and then, a good emperor rises to power and ends the corruption of his predecessors.

Near the conclusion of the Empire's existence, a series of inept rulers failed to keep the growing number of dangers under control.

Dishonest and controlling leaders disregarded Senate recommendations. The hostile Senate collaborated against the leaders and never made beneficial empire decisions.

The Praetorian Guard were the imperial bodyguards, but they, too, succumbed to the euphoria of absolute authority.

They settled on a candidate for Emperor and then frequently assassinated him.

This level of corruption persisted right up until Rome's demise.

The timeframe we live in today has all the characteristics of society that the Roman Empie had when that Republic was destroyed.

End of Civilization

The signs of the collapse of Civilization are everywhere; it is not just here in America but in the World.

Luciferian derangement is operating at total capacity as the warning signs cry out to us; A war between good and evil is playing out.

Narcissism is Rising! Normalcy is forsaken, and the bizarre and unnatural are embraced and considered the norm by many.

No major city in America is exempt from the rise of crime and Lawlessness.

There is no safe place to escape the dangers of malignant narcissists any longer in America, as lunatics roam the streets, malls, hospitals, churches, schools, and in every facet of society.

Greed and power have taken over many of those in leadership.

First and foremost, it is the general departure from reality; thus, common sense appears to have been banished from the culture.

Many consider the Constitution and laws put into place by the forefathers no longer exist today because society is too advanced.

Nothing is left but impending danger when God is rejected in the World.

Narcissism is flourishing in humanity and is welcomed. Once considered a mental illness, Narcissistic individuals control the planet and set a precedent for all of us to live by.

Civilization is nearing its end, and the insane now have the keys to the asylum; we are slowly watching humanity crumble and plunge into deep darkness as the light is extinguished.

Just as the Days of Noah and Lot were, it is with America and the World today.

Jesus and the prophets foretold everything happening in our World today, but sadly most ignore the prophecy.

As God said in (Genesis 6), Because the wickedness was so great, it sorrowed Him that He created humankind.

Undoubtedly, He looks down upon His creation today and says the same thing.

God will not allow the wickedness we see today to go on much longer. As Lawlessness and depravity overtake the World, We have been weighed in the balance and found wanting.

13

Faithfully Dedicated

Never have we witnessed such an outpouring of support and dedication for what a branch of their new religion is now.

The "Spirit of the Age" is its founder and is moving mighty as it draws the faithful into its movement.

People from all walks of life are excited about this new worship form. Businesses, Sports, Corporations, Academia, Hollywood, Government, and Churches have joined the Fellowship.

Their apostles and prophets are dedicated to ensuring their converts grow in large numbers.

With such a large magnitude of this movement, be assured that this is not just a phase or trend that will pass; quite the contrary, it is promoted by a hierarchy and considered a "special class."

There will be no "ban or lockdowns" on this unique form of their religion as it's converts genuflect to its Alter of Worship, ensuring the Earth is saturated with its New Doctrine.

This New Fellowship of believers is faithfully committed and has each other's backs as they grow in numbers daily.

They are a Committed Group, a Committed Church, and we are witnessing an actual branch of their religion act out their true purpose.

We are living in an "untrue" moment in America as the Spirit of the Age has become increasingly aggressive to reach the finish line in the completion of their Final World Empire. This new branch of their new religion introduced by the Spirit of the Age is a significant part of their plan.

Narcissism is Rising! We are watching in "Real Time" the End of Civilization as we know it.

While most Christians sit back in their comfort zone, watching their favorite movie, playing video games, and attending church on Sunday, a New Revival is disciplining many into their religious movement.

This new worship movement is a religious cult dedicated to their new doctrine of Transgenderism.

This Movement is Moving forward and exuberantly drawing many converts into their established doctrine.

Drag queens have announced on camera that they are Culture, Art and are here to stay.

The audience's applause is outgoing and spectacular to celebrate this new and growing movement.

As mentioned, celebrating their religious cult is embraced in all facets of society.

They will indeed accomplish their goals in this new movement. It is impossible for them not to when you have one side fiercely dedicated, unified, and fighting for their cause and the other side too busy to get involved or just hoping it will all pass away one day. I am sorry; that is delusional thinking!

We are daily witnessing a secular world in decline. Only one side matters now, and the powers that be agree they no longer need a country like the America we once were familiar with.

That "Old Country" stands in the way of their New World.

They want a New Order, hence, New World Order.

"Build Back Better" is the slogan, and that is what they are doing, at least in their eyes.

The secular world is being transformed into the Beast System.

A new religion is here to stay. The masses are dedicated to their cause.

The rejection of reality is being played out in most of humanity.

The ancient texts hold the "key" to revealing the "Truth" of what to expect from conditions on Earth in society just before and during the Final World Empire.

A new religion has surfaced; this is not the time to ignore reality. It would help if you decided what to do if a "mob" comes knocking on your door, as they did to Lot on his Day.

As mentioned, we are halfway through the establishment of the Final World Empire, to many, known as; The Great Reset, Agenda 2030, New World Order, or Global Government.

Because they rejected the "Truth," God sent them strong delusions.

(Revelation 13:4,8)

And they worshipped the Beast saying, who is like unto the Beast? Who can make war with him?

And all that dwell upon the Earth shall worship the Beast, whose name is not written in the book of life of the Lamb slain from the foundations of the world.

14

You Will Own Nothing and be Happy.

A nightmarish description by the authoritarian members of the WEF often promotes their plans for the Great Reset. You will own nothing and be happy, they tell us.

The influential members of the WEF, U.N., IMF, and others are currently setting the stage for the Great Reset in the Final World Empire.

A part of their Agenda:

It will seem different, but you can still be happy without owning a home, car, household machines, and clothes.

You will discover outgoing generosity while living under a New Regime.

Transportation, housing, and other daily essentials are available.

Another party will utilize our vacant area whenever we aren't using it; therefore, we don't pay rent in our town.

Individuals will allow others to hold business meetings in their living room when they are not home. Seclusion is no longer possible.

Just reading this information gives us a clear understanding of their goals for ordinary people.

Every country must transfer the oil, gas, and technology industries, suggesting that the United States and China must work together on this plan.

The U.N. has aggressively opposed property rights for many years and has long been a party to the fight against property rights.

According to the U.N., owning property and personal possessions is wealth anyone cannot hold, and it is a prime illustration of Social Justice.

Private ownership of land and privacy will be prohibited during the Great Reset, the WEF Global Future Council predicts.

Consumer everyday items will not be regarded as private property.

According to the WEF, if this scenario is correct, people will have to rent and borrow their daily requirements from the government, which will become the sole provider of goods and services.

The supply of goods will be distributed in line with a social credit system.

There will no longer be conventional shopping, and individual purchases will close.

Every personal move will be traced digitally, and all manufacturing will be subject to specifications of renewable energy and a sustainable environment.

In a sustainable environment, the food supply will be primarily vegetarian.

The state will provide basic housing, food, and transportation in an authoritarian economic market, and the rest will be borrowed from the state.

The utilization of natural resources will be reduced to the lowest level.

To deter the production and use of carbon dioxide, a global organization would put a very high price and tax on carbon emissions.

Summary of the WEF Agenda for a New World:

- **People will have no ownership over anything. Products are provided at no cost to consumers or must be borrowed from the state.**
- **The intake of meat will be cut down significantly.**
- **America will cease to be a superpower, and a small group of countries will exercise totalitarian control over the world.**
- **Instead of organ donors, 3D-printed organs will be used.**
- **Billions of people will be forced to seek safety in other countries.**
- **Humans can prepare to travel to Mars and begin their search for life beyond Earth.**
- **A sky-high global price will be set to discourage carbon emissions.**
- **There will be a severe strain on Western principles and their way of life.**

The Contributors to the Great Reset during the Final World Empire's ideology they could create a disease-free New World.

Because of advances in biotechnological manufactured organs, life expectancy they believe will improve significantly, and they will obtain immortality with tailored genetic-based medical therapies.

As Narcissism is Rising in the souls of wealthy ruling-class officials, the ideology of their "Great Reset" in a "2030 Final World Empire," Artificial Intelligence will make death and disease a thing of the past.

Companies are currently speeding up the biotechnology process in competing for the solution to eternal life.

For those who can no longer find work in the new digital market, a worldwide basic income and a vow to transform ordinary people into godlike beings is quite enticing.

To guarantee a universal base income would result from a wage difference leveling to move forward economically.

A cashless society would require monetary transfers from the state by technical procedures.

Each consumer purchase will be registered in the new digitalization of a cashless world.

As a result of this new digitalization, the government will use its totalitarian authority to administer, in detail, how each person spends their money down to the last cent.

In their cashless world, global income will impose a social credit system to identify those unwelcome and discipline unacceptable behavior.

The World Economic Forum has not presented any reliable evidence on its website which indicates who the New Leaders will be in their remarkably disease-free and immortal godlike free New World.

Each individual must decide for themselves. Is there any concrete notion that the powerholders under this new system will show benevolence toward the "useless eaters" or "deplorable" as ordinary people are labeled?

Where is the logic to believe the ruling class is serious about turning the "commoners" into godlike beings, and why would they distribute their Al with the "ruthless eaters" of the world?

In logically assessing the dream the hierarchy plans to carry out in their Utopian Empire, we must conclude whether they plan to share the planet with those they deem "unacceptable" and "subservient."

Why was a monument called the "Georgia Guidestones" erected? Engraved in their stone monument are the Ten Commandments for a New World, and the first says keeping the world's population under 500 million in balance with nature.

One must do their search for the Truth when hearing the preaching of the Social Justice gospel by the benefactors of the Great Reset.

Lurking in the shadows, behind their undertakings and pledges put out on certain official websites and social media by specific promoters of the "2030 New World" agenda, is a sinister scheme of eugenics, which is currently called "genetic engineering."

They have changed the name frequently in the past but are now out in the open on their true intentions, and as previously mentioned, Transhumanism is the outcome they envision.

They are all on board with this plan of merging humans with machines.

What is presented to the public is nothing more than a brutal onslaught on humanity in removing liberty and the dignity of every human being on planet Earth.

The technologies presented for the improvement and common good of the world are nothing more than an instrument to deceive the masses and, in the end, enslave the world.

As mentioned, we must access the reality of what we are told about a plan for a New Reset of the World.

Understanding the ancient texts predicted by the prophets and Jesus Himself about this coming Final World Empire will significantly inform, with knowledge, to the reader what to expect as we watch those events unfold.

It may also help for a better understanding to go back and review "chapter seven," Narcissism Rising!

(2 Timothy 3:13) Tell us: **Evil men and seducers will worsen as we see the Day approaching.**

The above scripture tells us what characteristics in much of society will be like just before the Tribulation begins and during that time frame. It describes Malignant Narcissistic individuals who are insane and live in an altered universe.

We are witnessing the formation of the Final World Empire, which, as mentioned, is the Great Reset. The promoters of this Empire are working diligently to have it completed by 2030 or sooner.

According to the scriptures, this Final World Empire is the Beast System of Revelation 13.

The promoters of this New Empire are all out in the open. It is no secret who they are, as they now openly tell us of their plans for us.

The Ruling Emperor of this New World Order is waiting to come center stage. It will be when God says it is time for him to be revealed publicly.

There are still some events that must take place before he arrives.

15

Narcissists are Spiritually Dark

Within the past few years, we have witnessed how spiritually defective some Narcissistic leaders can be. It is because they have no moral compass to guide them.

Narcissists believe they are flawless individuals. They make promises to improve society, yet, instead of improvement, we find hardship.

(Proverbs 28:12) "When the wicked rule, the people mourn; they suffer violence and injustice, and have bitter cause for complaint and lamentation."

Narcissistic Traits in Some Bureaucrats

- **They Lie; Everything they say is a lie, even when it sounds promising; it's a lie. They have to lie to cover their last talk because it is a lie.**
- **Self-Absorbed – It's all about them, their plans, policies, schemes, and plots. Dissent is not welcome.**
- **Manipulators – They are expert manipulators and manipulate their way into policy making.**

- They have no empathy and lack the public's concerns and compassion.
- They live in a delusional universe. They have a warped mindset and are out of touch with reality.
- They are controllers, and it is their primary trait besides pride. They want to control the narrative, situation, agenda, and everyone on Earth.
- They create chaos and then devise a solution to fix the problem.
- They only have evil intent toward humanity.
- They are hard taskmasters. Ordinary people are oppressed and live in fear and anxiety.
- They are void of doing what is morally right for the people they are supposed to represent.
- They oppose the good and choose the wrong in delicate decision-making. They are anti-God and do everything they can to oppose the natural laws of God and nature.

Trust the Maestro

We all trusted the experts during a pandemic. Yet, things turned out to be the opposite of what was told.

- Trust the Maestro: Playgrounds were shut down, and walks on the beach would get you arrested.
- Trust the Maestro: Many lost their employment.
- Trust the Maestro: Small businesses were lost.
- Trust the Maestro: Wear a mask, maybe two at a time.
- Trust the Maestro: Children could not play together at school and were seated in cubicles.
- Trust the Maestro: It lasted two years after being told only fifteen days to flatten the curb.
- Trust the Maestro: They told us you will be virus free if you get vaccinated.

- **Trust the Maestro: Get two or three vaccines and four boosters.**
- **Trust the Maestro: You still get the virus, but it is only mild.**
- **Trust the Maestro: The vaccine is safe.**
- **Trust the Maestro: The Truth finally arrives.**
- **Trust the Maestro: Sudden Death Syndrome.**
- **Trust the Maestro: Did we get the truthful facts?**

Falsehood is everywhere. We have reached a point where It will be wise for each individual to evaluate on their own what is Truth and False.

Narcissistic individuals are spiritually dark, and when they present a solution to the masses about specific events and situations, one must decide what to believe.

Hopefully, past experiences have served as a wake-up call to many.

16

The Final World Empire & Church Age Ends

The Final World Empire is the last form of Gentile World Government that will rule the world before the New Age begins, called the Millennium.

Many horrific events are predicted to occur during this Final World Empire, but as mentioned, the Rapture of the Church will happen first at the close of this church age.

The word "church" in Greek means "called out." It is not a religion, mainline denomination, or building; it means those committed to Jesus.

The first Church was started in Antioch and was where the first disciples of Jesus Christ were called Christians.

"Christian" is not someone who has a religion but a "life transformation," which is referred to in **(John 3)** as "Born Again."

This current "church age" we live in started on the Day of

Pentecost, Fifty days after the crucifixion of the Lord Jesus, and will end at the Rapture.

The reason for the "church age" is to give every individual on Earth time to repent of their sins and make Jesus Christ Lord and Savior, to be Born Again, and tell those that will listen to the "Good News" that Jesus will deliver them from their sins, and coming soon.

God is Merciful and wants everyone to be spared from eternal damnation, so He sent His Son to die on the cross for us. It is up to each of us to make the right decision about who we will serve.

When the "church age" ends, the Tribulation will begin, and God's Judgments will fall on the Earth.

Conditions on Earth During Final World Government

As mentioned in the Book of Revelation, Daniel and other books describe conditions on Earth during the Final World Empire, which will usher in the Tribulation.

Keep in mind that the prophetic warnings have been out for centuries. God is merciful but also a "Just" God, meaning He will not allow evil to continue forever.

- **The Church's Rapture occurs at the end of the "church age."**
- **The Time of Jacobs Trouble Begins (Tribulation) begins.**

It is referred to in the ancient texts, Jacobs Trouble, because God called His Jewish people Jacob.

As mentioned, during the Final World Empire, the Tribulation is a time of tremendous pain and suffering, so much so that scriptures tell us if God did not shorten the Days, no flesh would be spared, but for His elect sake (Israel), those days will be shortened.

This timeframe we live in is also called The Times of the Gentiles. It is a long period that first began with the Babylonian captivity of Juda, a province in Israel under King Nebuchadnezzar. It will end with the destruction of Gentile World power at the coming of the Lord Jesus in Glory (Rev 19:11,21).

During this Final World Empire and into the Tribulation period, tremendous judgments from God will fall upon Earth dwellers.

Those Judgments will affect the world, but primarily in the Middle East. It is because God turned His attention toward the Jewish people once the church age ended, but the rest of the world will suffer also.

The Book of Revelation tells us that God pours His Judgments out by Seven Seals, Trumpets, and Vials.

As mentioned, the world will be affected by those cataclysmic Judgments.

God will pour out His Wrath on all who refuse His "gift "of Salvation, which is the reason for the Tribulation period.

For those whose names are not written in the "Book of Life," the scriptures tell us, is the reason for those Judgments to occur.

God will chasten His Jewish remnant in Israel so they will cry out to God for Mercy after intense suffering and persecution by the Antichrist world leader. Then, their eyes will be open, and they will realize that Jesus is the true Messiah they have waited for.

The Seven-Year Tribulation will begin with the signing of the covenant by the Antichrist with many. He will then break the covenant in the middle of the seven years, and those last three-and-one-half years will be when God's full Wrath is poured out upon all humanity.

The Battle of Armageddon will commence at the end of the Tribulation.

The Earth will then be cleansed, and Jesus will Return to set up His Kingdom, the Millianum lasting 1,000 years.

The Final World Empire will not be the "Utopia" the ruling class envisioned, but something entirely different from their expectations.

17

Reprobates & Normalcy Rejected

Narcissistic individuals are Reprobates, and according to the scriptures, anyone who hears the Truth rejects it and embraces the negative has such traits (Romans 1:18).

An excellent example of a Reprobate is someone who suppresses the Truth by their wicked actions and intentionally chooses to do the wrong; it is the mindset of society today.

Normalcy no longer exists in this country, and the world is upside down; in fact, a Narcissists-Reprobate mindset in society is engulfing the planet. Like a spider spins its web and gets bigger, it is in humanity today.

Normalcy is no longer accepted, and unnatural change is preferred.

A clear indication that End Times are upon us is when we see a depraved mindset accepted by most of the population in the country.

According to the ancient texts, when we reach this era, it indicates only one thing, "The Day of the Lord" (Tribulation) is about to begin, but first, the vanishing of God's Church occurs.

A True End Time sign is when we see a negative change embraced mainly for the first time since God destroyed the world in flood on Noah's Day.

Normalcy Rejected

Remember that the negative we see is widely accepted in the population, and even parents allowing their children as young as a seven-eight-year-old to decide to have their bodies mutilated and put on puberty blockers is differently a clear indication God's Wrath is about to be poured out upon an unregenerate world.

At one time, America was a Christian nation.

We now live in a God-Forsaken World except for a small remnant of true believers, and because of this, serious thought should be considered on what side each of us will associate with.

In other words, there is no longer a middle ground for us to relax in and hope conditions improve and time is delayed for us to continue enjoying all the world's pleasures.

I hate to disappoint you, but it is not going to happen.

What we have allowed as a society is turning our heads at the onslaught of evil engulfing us, taking it a step further, accepting it, and remaining in the silent majority; Normalcy is never coming back despite who leads the country.

We have allowed everything to happen in this country. We have been "Weighed in the Balance and Found Wanting." Conditions in this country and the world will not improve but deteriorate.

We have passed the era of debate and trying to reason with others; that phase is gone.

For those who aren't sure of what to expect or don't understand what is happening around us, allow me to explain.

At this current time in history, our country and the world are being transformed into "The Final World Government." As mentioned, currently, we are over halfway to the completion.

Serious thoughts about more important things than our everyday schedule must be considered.

The scriptures are clear about this era we currently live in. That is, "He who is righteous, let him be righteous still. Him who is filthy, let him be filthy still. (Revelation 22:11).

The above verse tells us that when we have reached this point, each individual will be one or the other, depending on your belief. There is no longer time to procrastinate.

Hopefully, everyone will make the right decision and get right with God by accepting God's Salvation through Jesus, His Son, before it is too late.

As we progress into "The Final World Empire," conditions continue to deteriorate; an excellent example is that the unrighteous no longer seek individual rights; they have them.

The situation has escalated into those that are righteous are now being policed by the unrighteous, and the hate being presented to the righteous has become dangerous.

They do not want to share the planet with anyone who disagrees.

Conditions have reached an overwhelming hostility toward those who do not embrace the trends of the culture.

As mentioned, the negative is accepted by most of the population, and the normal is rejected.

Now that we have entered this era in society, one of two things will occur in the country and world; It is either Revival or Bust.

I have studied Prophetic texts for over four decades, and nowhere have I found that Revival will take place, but conditions continue to deteriorate in the World.

The only time revival will occur is during the Tribulation when the angel announces to the world the everlasting gospel. The Two witnesses appear, and the 144,000 Jewish evangelist witness to the

Jewish people in Israel and those Gentiles that have never heard the message.

So, we must quickly decide what is most important to us.

Civilization is collapsing as we enter The Final World Empire (Great Reset) and see clear indications we are approaching a troublesome time ahead with horrific and dreadful events.

18

A Dark Regime

When the Apostle John had a Devine Visitation from the ascended Lord Jesus in His Kingly appearance, he was banished to the Isle of Patmos because he was part of the 12 Apostles that walked with Jesus during His earthly ministry.

John was the only Apostle not martyred, so he could write the Book of Revelation as a warning for all who have eyes and ears to hear the message.

As mentioned, Daniel the Prophet was told to write the things he was shown in a book as a warning.

Based on extensive research in the ancient texts and geopolitical observation, and what other biblical researchers believe, our nation and planet are on the precipice of entering the completion of the Final World Empire.

(Daniel 7, 11) Saw this Final World Empire as the Fourth Beast rising, and when he was shown this extraordinary sight, it was so dreadful he fainted and was sick for many days because of the horror he witnessed.

The Revised Roman Empire will be the regime Earth's inhabiters will live under.

It will be brutal to live under, and individuals are not allowed to make their own choices in conducting their lives, as once they were.

The policies, rules, and laws set before them will be ruthless, and anyone that does not comply will be dealt with harshly.

Reeducation camps will no doubt be set up for problematic people.

Consider, If you will, Malignant Narcissists will rule with an iron fist in this Final Global World.

Earth's inhabiters will face beatings, torture, starvation, and fatal cruelties if they are uncooperative with the authorities.

There is no regard for human life during this time, and ordinary people are serfs to the system.

Commoners will be used only to serve and for the pleasure of the hierarchy.

There will be only two classes of people under this dark regime: the upper class and the lower rank.

Under this Revised Final Roman Empire, slave labor will abound as was under Rome before it fell.

The Revised Roman Empire will extend to other countries; as the scripture tells us, all the world is under this system.

Anyone who has studied ancient history knows how cruel the imperial form of Rome was back on Jesus' Day.

Comparing that ancient time to what conditions will be during the Revised Roman Empire will be no comparison.

It is why Daniel fainted when he saw the vision shown to him by God of this fourth Beast, The Final World Empire.

As mentioned, this Final World Government comprises Ten Regions, and the world is divided into those Ten Areas.

The Antichrist rules over these Ten Regions.

Today's technology will make it impossible for anyone who tries to "flee" the Beast system under this dark regime.

Each person on Earth will have a digital ID. Currently, it is being formulated.

Drones will be used to track those who try to escape.

Satan is thrown down to the Earth (**Revelation 12:9**) during this time. He has great Wrath because he knows his time is short.

As you read along, I hope you can come to grips with how horrifying conditions on Earth are under this dark regime during this time.

As bad as things are already, nothing can compare with the terrifying experiences people on Earth will experience at the Close of Time under The Final World Empire.

God said He would shorten the days under the Beast System; otherwise, no one would survive.

The same plagues that fell in Egypt during Moses's time will be what falls upon the Earth, and more added.

The ancient texts tell us millions will die because of plagues and pestilence that engulf the planet.

There is nowhere to hide or escape the Judgments coming.

Ensuring you are right with God before these events begin is our Hope.

Famine is one of those plagues; we will explore that in the following chapters.

Death will be everywhere. Mobs, gangs, and looting will be in the cities, suburbs, and countryside.

Medicine and healthcare will not be available as we are accustomed to.

Those obedient to the regime are the only ones who will receive treatment.

Earthquakes such as the world has never experienced are coming.

Suppose you have not already read about such a time coming, and God Himself has declared these Prophecies will be fulfilled. In that case, it is there for anyone interested in their future and the future of loved ones to get familiar with the Prophecies in the Bible.

The coming Dark Regime under The Final World Empire is a time in history never before seen. So great evil and cruelty humanity will experience, Jesus tells His disciples to beware of deception because it will be so great that even His "Elect" (Israel) can be deceived.

The following chapters will explore the coming "Lamentations and Woes" the World will experience during the last Seven Years of this Age, Tribulation, under The Final World Empire.

19

The Seven Seals Open

The viewpoint is in Heaven, where John the Apostle was shown the scroll sealed with seven seals opening by the only One Worthy to open the scroll, Jesus, the Lamb that was slain, but now in all His Glory and Power.

The Four Horsemen ride throughout the Earth during what Jesus referred to in Matthew 24 as, The Beginning of Sorrows.

First Seal: Rider on the White Horse

(Revelation 6:1-2) The verse tells us, The Rider on the White Horse conquers all.

As mentioned, Tribulation gateways seem to be opening. The Rider on the White Horse appears to be seeping through those open gateways advancing his destruction upon Earth.

The Rider on The White Horse, The Final World Empire Conquering the World.

This Final World Empire cannot happen overnight but has already begun its organization as the rulers of the World are forming this Empire.

The Rider on the White Horse is conquering all traditions, standards, morals, principles, customs, and laws of God and nature our culture is familiar with.

The Horsemen is not conquering all at once but in stages.

He knows we are human and is conquering "covertly," so humanity is slowly conditioned to accept the "new norms" presented to them by this devilish Rider.

The Rider is a deceiver, destroying and dismantling everything and anyone in his path.

The Rider on the White Horse has begun his ride across a once-free and prosperous nation, America.

His job is to conquer each territory he enters, as Satan is the mastermind behind this Rider.

The devil believes he can convert all the World to himself and anxiously awaits his Empire, the Fourth Beast (Daniel 7).

The prophecies will be fulfilled about establishing The Final World Empire and all the horror contributing to this Global Government; the Rider on the White Horse ensures this happens.

This Rider is tearing apart individuals and families, and he has conquered many churches that once believed in and followed the Gospel of Jesus Christ.

There has been no resistance to this Rider on the White Horse; instead, a Welcome mat has been laid down for him as he trots across America.

As he patrols the land, many have applauded his conquest of the nation in all the destruction and dismantling.

Many Christians celebrate his entrance into a once Christian Nation. They are delighted with his conquest of morals, the family, schools, churches, and government because they are deceived.

The Watchmen have vanished, and the Alarm Bells no longer ring as a "Warning" to all, WAKE UP, WAKE UP, Destruction is here, and Civilization is collapsing!

It is a Prophecy being fulfilled; it's called "APOSASTY" in the Bible and the "Laodicean Lukewarm Church" that Jesus Himself said, He would spew them out.

The Rider on the White Horse's main conquest was and is the Church. He is nearly complete in achieving this goal.

The Rider has deceived many that wear the label Christian.

A small remnant of True Believers remains steadfast in the faith. They have a strong foundation on which they stand; Jesus is still their Lord, Savior, and Soon Coming King. This Rider cannot conquer them.

The job of this Horsemen is to conquer the entire planet. He has cast his dark web of deceit over the World, and because they don't have any substance, no moral compos to guide them, and no firm foundation to stand on, they are defeated.

Those that have all the above and are fully awake; warned the onlookers, sounding the alarm bells warning, "Danger is Approaching, Danger is Coming; yet, it was ignored, and they walked away laughing, scoffing, name-calling, a religious nut.

So here we are; it has all come to pass, and the scriptures are being fulfilled, and the onlookers remain in their dark trance, the web of deceit the Rider on the White Horse has cast his spell, and they are conquered.

The moral decline in the culture is a significant achievement in Rider's Conquest.

This Fourth Beast World Empire (The Great Reset), Jesus and the Prophets warned us will happen, and the Horsemen on the White Horse is ensuring that!

The Rider has driven God out of the land because society does not want Him. Instead, just as the scripture tells us, they will celebrate and welcome another prince; he is the Beast, the Antichrist of Revelation 13.

The Beast gets all his power from Satan in the unseen realm.

The Rider has driven God from the culture and substituted a shift into an erroneous belief system the public embraces, and it is anything Unnatural, Anti-God, Bad, and Despicable.

As the Horsemen stampedes across the Country and World, he is responsible for the chaos he creates in conquering and establishing his Great Reset, the Final World Empire.

He presents as an angel of light, casting his spell to give the masses a delusional reality of promises to improve the planet and their future.

The spirit of the Antichrist rides the White Horse as he conquers the World. He knows those supporting his coming World Ruler over the Final Empire.

A shift is taking place as the transformation of America is nearing completion.

The Rider on the White Horse occasionally gallops into the shadows to regroup and scheme his next conquest.

As mentioned, he works in stages so the public can slowly be conditioned into his delusional methods.

The Horsemen laugh gleefully as he casts deceit over the hearts and minds of a generation of people. He is proud of his conquering!

The Rider shoots his fiery darts with the bow he received in conquering into the minds of his victims as it paralyzes their thinking, and they accept the unnatural instead of the natural things in life.

When the Antichrist World Dictator comes onto the World stage, he will have no problem deceiving the World. It is because the Rider on the White Horse is going before him, conquering the souls and minds of society with an antichrist spirit.

A deceiving spirit will condition the World, so they will believe the "lie" the Narcissistic, Reprobate World leader presents.

As mentioned, the World will not suddenly be transformed into the Final Beast World Empire, but in "stages," as this is the job of the Rider on the White Horse.

In (Matthew 13:10-12) Jesus's disciples came to Him and asked

Him, "Why do you speak in parables when teaching the crowd? He replies, "Because you have been given the keys to unlock the mysteries of the heavenly kingdom, while they have not. The above verse refers to all who follow Jesus Christ and understand His speech. The others do not hear what He is saying because they choose not to.

The point is, As the Rider on the White Horse continues conquering humanity's minds, souls, and lives, they choose to follow this World system where Satan is the ruler. Therefore, they do not hear the warnings; they are unaware of the danger this Rider on the White Horse does, and just like a frog put in cold water to boil and slowly, the water gets hotter, it is unaware until it is too late.

The above illustration represents how The Rider conquers the masses as the White Horse gallops worldwide. They are slowly deceived as he offers all the World's pleasures, unnatural behaviors, and negativity.

Most of the World's humanity is unaware of the current events in the land, and the White Horse Rider has deceived them and cast his spell of delusion to believe his lies.

The moral decline in the World is growing increasingly wicked as each day passes.

There is no doubt about this; America and the World at this time are as, The Days of Noah and Lot.

If you don't recognize this, it may be time to do a reality check.

Jesus said this last generation would be like the Days of Noah and Lot.

Here we are, living in modern-day Sodom and Gomorra.

When the Rider on the White Horse sends the "mob" to your front door, trying to break it open as they did at Lot's house, will you hand your children over to them?

Other Conquering Methods of the Rider on the White Horse:

- The increasing intolerance and hostility toward Christians
- The radical movement of specific groups who want to shut down anyone with a different opinion.
- Everyone on Earth is given a digital identity complete with a QR code connected to their medical information, with the United Nations and World Health Organization overseeing their digital money.
- The WHO is laying the groundwork for a unified global government (under the sway of the WEF). A plot of affluent autocrats has usurped power in several countries governments.
- In recent years, due to widespread fear and concern of impending public health emergencies, the general population has consciously decided to put their faith in the government (not trusting God) beginning with Covid-!9, and dishonesty has reached epidemic proportions throughout the planet.
- With artificial intelligence on par with human intelligence, it is now feasible for the False Prophet to create an image of the Beast and give it the ability to converse, just as the Bible foretold would occur.
- Just as the Days of Noah are similar to modern-day America regarding the corruption of all flesh and the fact that the planet is filled with such criminal activity and tyranny as (11 Timothy 3:13) tells us, a shocking increase in spiritual darkness covers the Earth.

The Antichrist spirit has blanketed the World, and it is the cause of such grotesque darkness; the Antichrist spirit rides the White Horse in its conquest.

The White Horse Rider

As mentioned, the World will be divided into Ten Regions, with a King over each region, forming a One-World Final

Empire.

The Rider on the White Horse will stampede over everything in its path as the Fourth Revised Final Roman Empire is formed.

Once the World is split into Ten regions, with a King over each area, they will combine into trading block regions, forming an Economic Final World Empire.

When the Narcissistic, Reprobate Antichrist comes onto the World stage, he will change the laws and rules and combine the Ten regional trading block regions into a dark political regime, The Final End Time World Government.

Three countries already merged, called the North American Union (NAU).

They are Canada, the United States, and Mexico. It is also called the USMCA.

What makes this so unique:

A USMCA Super Railway was created on April 14, 2023, becoming the first freight railway to connect the United States, Mexico, and Canada. This supply chain is crucial to the North American Free Trade Agreement (NAFTA).

A step toward one of the Ten Kings appearing is the unification of the three North American countries into a single economic union and a regel trading block.

As it travels across the globe to complete its conquest, the Rider on the White Horse races toward the finish line, ushing in the Final One-World Empire.

Second Seal: Rider on Red Horse

(Revelation 6:3-4) The Rider on the Red Horse carries a "Great Sword" and is given authority to destroy peace in the World. It causes inhabitants of the Earth to murder one another.

In **(Matthew 24:6-7)** The verse suggests conflicts increase throughout the World due to turmoil in the nations as we move closer to the End of this Age.

Matthew describes a larger scale of Wars, such as World War 1 & World War 11, the Civil War, Iraq, and other major Wars. However, in the above verse in Revelation 6:3-4, John describes this as individuals killing one another in more minor disputes, such as mob violence, family disputes that turn violent, violent arguments between people, lone assailants, and more.

(Matthew 24) Jesus tells us we will hear of wars and rumors of wars. He implies we will listen to the sound of wars physically, with our hearing, and see new reports of wars elsewhere.

In other words, more minor violent crimes are happening in our streets, and at the same time, around the World in more significant and prominent wars.

The Red Horse, the Greek word John uses for red, is *"purrs or pyros," which* refers to the color of fire. It is not the common Greek word for red *(authors), which* John uses but a specified term that John suggests fieriness or flickering reds, oranges, and yellows like a flame of fire. Its color implies heat and ferocity like an out-of-control wildfire.

The Rider on the Red Horse carries a "great sword." The translation of this "great sword" is not a military weapon but a shorter sword or long knife comparable to a dagger, a blade utilized for preparing sacrifice or animal slaughter; it also implies an executioner's blade.

The "sword" is described as "great" and is significantly larger than average and successful at completing the job.

"And power was given to all four Horseman to slay with the sword, hunger, and Death, according to **(Revelation 6:8).**

A "great sword" is equivalent to a lethal weapon with exceptional effectiveness.

The flaming Red Horse, vast sword, and unrelenting aggression of the Rider on the Red Horse are frightening symbols of growing and unstoppable conflict and chaos. Humanity is terrified of this Horseman.

Violent crimes such as murders are happening daily on America's streets. At the same time, more significant wars are occurring in Ukraine; we hear reports of China possibly invading Taiwan and even hearing of a possible Nuclear War. In America daily, we hear of such unending violence in the streets. Why would anyone at this time recommend "defund police"?

Children are no longer safe to play in their yards or playgrounds.

The Rider on the Red Horse, just as the Rider on the White Horse, both seem to be seeping through Tribulation Portals. Narcissism is Rising in the streets of America! And there are yet two more horsemen to mount their steeds, leave their stalls and start racing across the World.

Third Seal: Rider on the Black Horse

(Revelation 6:5-6) The Rider on the Black Horse does not carry a weapon, but he does have a "set of balances in his hand."

The Greek word used for the black color of this horse is *"gnopho."* It refers to darkness, gloom, and blackness.

The above verse in Revelation 6:5-6 tells us it will cost one day's wage for a loaf of bread and one day's pay for a ration of barley.

The Set of Balances the Rider carries suggests Inflation and Famine.

Food scarcity directly results from the previous two Riders, Conquest and War.

The Conquering of the White Horse Rider in the farm belt of

America; The Burning Down of Some of the significant chicken factories in the Country (no one knows the mystery behind the fires).

The slaughtering of cattle, hogs, and other farm animals because farmers do not have the fertilizers to grow their crops and feed the animals.

China, as well as Bill Gates, have bought up most of the farm-land in America. Perhaps there is a sinister reason for this?

As far as Inflation and Famine, as this Rider on the Black Horse represents, Here in America, it initially started with the "supply chain."

That was the first thing reported. We no longer hear about this. Yet, the price of groceries has skyrocketed.

Inflation has reached an all-time high and continues to get worse.

(Revelation 6:5-6) Also, say, "Hurt, not the oil and the wine."

The above verse tells us that food prices will rise eight times higher, yet luxury items, oil, and wine will remain relatively cheap.

A trip to the grocery store today shows us how high the prices have already doubled and tripled in some commodities and will increasingly worsen.

As we can see, the Rider on the Black Horse and the other two Riders have already seeped through the "Tribulation Portals.

Once the Four Horsemen are given the go-ahead to Race through the Earth, causing despair, destruction, and Death to its max, conditions in the World will be so bad that people will commit suicide. Death will be everywhere, as we will see in the last Rider of These Four Horsemen, which is the most dread-ful.

Fourth Seal: Rider on the Pale Horse

(Revelation 6:7-8) When the Lamb opens the "Fourth Seal,"

John the Apostle sees a pale-colored horse. The Rider on this horse is called Death, and the scriptures tell us Hades (hell) follows this Rider.

Some translators say Death and Hades ride together on this horse, and others suppose hell follows on another horse. Either way, the verse tells us that all killed by this Rider called Death will go to Hades because hell follows this last Rider to gather all the souls of those killed.

This Rider was given authority over one-fourth of the World to kill people using wars, famines, plagues, and with wild beasts of the Earth.

The Pale horse that Death rides is a corpse-like sickly color, and some translators describe it as an ashen (pale greenish-gray) horse.

The previous three Horsemen caused much havoc over the Earth and contributed to the Rider on the Pale horse, Death.

The Rider on the White Horse conquers by destruction, as it dismantles the foundations of the countries of the World, changing rules and laws to mutilate very young children who are not cognitively developed to make decisions for themselves, creating havoc on the food supply chain, and energy system, academia, medical, dismantling the military making the Country vulnerable to its enemies, removing borders and so much more.

The Rider on the Red Horse carries a "great sword," He kills locally, as violent crime is rising daily. It would help if officials put into law a guard at every school in America, both private and public. At one time in our Country, children were considered the bedrock of society. The Rider on the Red Horse is also responsible for wars, and he causes Death everywhere he rides.

The Rider on the Black Horse causes starvation, famine, and

inflation. Farmers cannot feed their animals because they lack fertilizer and other essential resources. Grocery products are rising alarmingly; the supply chain is damaged, and inflation is off the charts.

As mentioned, the first three Riders help to aid the fourth and final Rider, Death. Yet, this Rider has not left his stall as the others are seeping through Tribulation portals; the Rider on the Pale Horse is waiting for the "set time" to Ride in "full fury" with no restraints.

Because of so many plagues, wars, and famines, one-fourth of the Earth's population, according to scripture, will die from the Rider on the Pale Horse.

One-fourth of the Earth's population equals over one billion people; North America, South America, and Brazil are equal to over one billion.

When the Rider on the Pale Horse is given the command to Ride in all his fury over the Earth, reaping Death everywhere he goes with hell following, it will be the "First Judgment Wave" to strike the Earth.

It has never happened in the pages of history yet, but when the Lamb opens this "Seal," it will be explosive, as **(Revelation 6:7-8)** tells us. The suffering and loss of life will be indescribable living under The Final World Empire.

Fifth Seal: Martyred Remnant

Jesus tells us that the Tribulation under the Final World Empire ruled by the Antichrist of Revelation 13 will be a time of unprecedented persecution for those who refuse to worship the image and refuse the Beast mark.

(Revelation 6:9-11) The Fifth Seal talks about thousands of souls under the altar in Heaven. These souls are gathered because they were martyred for their witness of Jesus and commitment to Him. They cry, asking Him, "How long must they wait until Christ avenges their blood on the Earth? Jesus instructs them to wait until the other servants are killed as they were. White robes were given to each of them.

The opening of this seal will be when the anti-christ agents search everywhere for new believers in Jesus Christ. They will be hunted down everywhere they suspect the Christians to be hiding. There will be few safe places; once captured, they are taken to detention centers and given a choice, take the mark or be executed.

Those that do not take the (Radio Frequency Identification Microchip) will be considered enemies of the new world system because they refuse to follow the guidelines and requirements given under the anti-christ regime.

This new "mark" will be to "seal" the souls of those who choose to follow satan. The anti-christ agents will force those they capture and anyone else to take the mark, and satan is the driving force behind it.

This persecution will be throughout the Tribulation, but will intensify at the mid-point, the last three and one-half years.

In (Isaiah 26:20-21) Is the prophecy of the Rapture, as the Lord shows His prophet Isaiah the Rapture, and then His wrath falls upon the Earth; once His people enter their chambers and close the door as that verse says, (the Rapture) God's terrible time of wrath falls upon the planet.

It is best to be prepared to escape God's coming wrath; Jesus Christ is your escape by trusting in His Salvation. There is no other way; He is the way, the Truth, and the life!

Think about the current spiritual Antichrist atmosphere in our World today. Given the Antichrist demonic allies crave power, control, and the lifeblood of Christ's family, I can comprehend how these saints of the Tribulation will experience intensified persecution.

The Anti-Christian campaign is advancing further than ever before in human history. Persecution seemed inconceivable a few years ago, but that has now changed. The forces of darkness are at work, poisoning people's minds with hate toward God's people. Currently, some openly advocate the murder of Godly people.

God was thrown out of Europe decades ago, and it seems they enjoy worshiping dark images.

The antichrist spirit is moving quickly worldwide, as many countries now openly have occultic ceremonies, including the United States. As mentioned, a great example:

- **The 2023 Superbowl halftime show was demonic and total depravity.**
- **The Grammys of 2023 took the initiative and lived up to their standing.**
- **At the Commonwealth Games in the United Kingdom in 2022, the organizers danced about in worship of a Beast as they rolled it out under the limelight. At the same time, they bowed down to honor the Beast while dancing seductively.**
- **The 2016 Tunnel Ceremony took 17 years to construct the largest tunnel project in history, which passes through the Swiss Alps. To commemorate the opening of the tunnel, a bizarre satanic ceremony was held, which was attended by numerous chiefs of state.**
- **The biggest Satanic convention Satan Con 2023, was held in Boston, MA. April 28-30.**
- **Satan after-school care clubs to condition the young in their impressionable years.**

The Antichrist spirit spreads Satanism worldwide as it roams about seeking whom it may devour, and TV programs such as Lucifer and Little Demon contribute to the sinister movement spreading its cloak of darkness across the World.

(Revelation 13:4) Warns us that all of Earth's inhabitants will worship the dragon (Satan) during the Tribulation. It is why we are already seeing the celebration and applauding of the audience, as it was at the Super Bowl halftime show that there were such loud cheers and applause that you could not hear the music, only the cheers. It should be a "wake-up" to most; sadly, the masses prefer the darkness.

It is why the above scripture points out to us that all Earth dwellers will worship the Beast, those that have taken the Antichrist's mark on the forehead or right hand.

If we are already seeing the celebration and welcoming of the worship of Satan at these games and elsewhere, do you think the Tribulation is far off and you will not see it in your lifetime?

If that is what you believe, sadly, you will probably be one who will run to the front lines to get the "Mark" when it is official. The digital ID and currency will arrive between 2023 - 2025 because the research appears accurate.

Those whose names are not written in the Book of Life, and Jesus was evident in (John 3), "You must be Born Again," to get your name written in that Book.

If the Tribulation is at our front door, and we are minutes before midnight, how much closer do you think the Rapture is?

As mentioned, everything predicted by the prophets and Jesus Himself will occur, and we are witnessing the preparations being put in place.

It will be tough being a believer during the Tribulation under the final World Empire; you will be martyred for your faith, but the good news is you go to Heaven. If you accept the "mark," you can buy and sell, but Jesus tells us you will be damned if you do. If you don't take it, you will not be able to buy the bare necessities to survive; It is the reason for the digital ID and currency for tracking.

(Revelation 20:4) Tells thousands, if not millions, will be killed for their faith and commitment to Jesus during the Tribulation under the Final World Empire. Beheading is how they will be martyred, as the above scripture is clear.

The souls under the altar as the fifth seal is open are part of those Tribulation saints that cry out to God for vengeance because of those who killed them on Earth. It will be a terrible time for those left on Earth because they chose to ignore the Truth and believe the Lie.

Those that don't abide by the rules and laws set forth by the Beast under his regime will be rounded up and sent to the camps.

I encourage you to research and get informed. Do what you can now while you still have time to gather information for yourself and learn. The time is late!

Sixth Seal: Catastrophic Judgments & Cosmic Terror

(Revelation 6:12-16) The events brought about by the opening of the Sixth Seal will send humanity running and hiding in dread.

Some of those events:

- **Massive and powerful earthquakes are felt worldwide.**
- **The Sun becomes Dark.**
- **The moon turns Blood Red.**
- **The heavens dissipate like a scroll when it is rolled up together.**
- **The earthquakes are so powerful they cause mountains and islands worldwide to move out of their place.**
- **Many earth dwellers run to the mountains to hide in dens and under the large rocks.**
- **The stars fall to the Earth.**

A massive earthquake will create a chain of disasters that will ultimately change the planet and the universe.

It will be an earthquake so great it will be felt worldwide, and the following tragedies will confirm ancient predictions about this time known as the Great Tribulation.

The magnitude of this earthquake predicted, and other earthquakes to follow, will make all other earthquakes before the Tribulation seem small.

All other earthquakes before will be like twenty-five-foot-high ocean waves washing ashore. In contrast, the vast quake predicted during this time will be like a tsunami that is 1,500 feet or higher, crashing ashore and traveling thousands of miles inland and killing everything in its path.

Following this terrifying event, the Sun will darken, and the moon will turn a blood-red color. The black Sun will be constrained by the passage of time because no one has ever experienced it. The event that will transpire with the Sun during this time will be an event no one up till this time has experienced.

The blood-red color of the moon will not be like the regular blood moons we have witnessed that are orangish with tan color hues. The blood moon during the Tribulation under the Final World Empire will be just as predicted; an indisputably blood-red color that will strike more terror into the hearts of Earth's inhabitants witnessing this event.

Such cosmic events will cause the heavens (universe) to roll up as a scroll.

During these cosmic catastrophes that will take place, the fear that already permeates the globe is going to intensify further with each event that occurs.

All these events that will fall upon the Earth during the Great Tribulation are God still trying to get the attention of humanity to turn to Him in sincere repentance.

Scientists and other world leaders will dismiss such cosmic events that everything happening is natural, and they have it all under control. They will deceive the people living on Earth, and sadly, they will believe them.

The Apostle John continues to explain in writings in Revelation he sees the stars falling from the sky. John explains all events as he sees them, and remember, he is doing his best as a first-century man to put into writing what he sees. The stars he sees falling are meteorites or comets that will cause significant damage to the planet. If a star ever fell to Earth, it would incinerate the Earth.

We are also told that the opening of the sixth seal will be so dreadful it will cause many earth dwellers to flee to the mountains and hide in the dens and rocks of the mountains. As mentioned, many wealthy people have bought underground bunkers for emergencies; there are also advanced underground tunnels leading to dwelling places for wealthy world leaders and elites.

They have created underground bunkers for storing food, seeds, and supplies. It is all for the globalist, of course.

The opening of the sixth seal will terrorize humanity all over the globe, and there are more judgments following, dreadful and gruesome.

20

Seventh Seal: 144,000 Jewish Evangelists Sealed & Trumpet Judgments.

(Revelation 8:1)

The 144,000 Jewish Evangelists are sealed as an angel is instructed to put God's divine seal on before the seventh seal is opened. Those sealed by the angel will be a witness for Jesus throughout the earth, especially to the Jewish nation of Israel.

Once they are sealed, a great assembly in Heaven gives praises in worship to Jesus, who is now in His Kingly character.

The Seventh Seal is broken, and a strange and unusual silence settles in Heaven for about one-half hour.

The Seventh Seal begins to present Seven Trumpets. After the opening of the prior Six Seals, there was a precise judgment that took place. Introducing the Seventh Seal will not result in the pronouncement of any particular judgment. The arrival of seven angels occurs, and each of them is given a trumpet, and after they sound the trumpet, a specific judgment occurs, making it a total of Seven Trumpet Judgments.

The number seven represents completion in scripture, and back in ancient biblical days, trumpets were blown to make announcements. The Seven Trumpets will sound to proclaim seven Trumpet Judgments.

After the Seven Trumpet Judgments occur, the last of God's judgments will follow with Seven Bowl (or vial) Judgments.

The Seventh Seal can be seen as an entrance or gateway because it does not have a single specific judgment associated with it (but rather several).

The Seventh Seal essentially ushers in the actual culmination of Judgments and the conclusion of the End of the Age before Jesus Returns to Set up His Kingdom.

First Trumpet Sounds:
(Revelation 8:7)

The First Trumpet sounds as the angel blows the Trumpet. People all across the earth will experience Hail and Fire mixed with Blood falling from the sky. It will be brimstone rain in the form of hailstones. It is the brimstone that fell from heaven on Sodom and Gomorrah. This plague causes one-third of the world's trees to be devoured by fire, eradicating all green grass. It is comparable to the seventh plague that visited Egypt during Moses's day. (Exodus 9:23-24)

Second Trumpet Sounds:
(Revelation 8:8-9)

The Second Trumpet sounds as the angel blows the Trumpet. Something that looks like a Great Mountain on fire falling from the sky lands in the Sea. It could be a supercharged asteroid that is burning and very hot. John is trying to describe as he is shown this Judgment. It causes one-third of the ocean to become blood, a third of all ships to be destroyed, and a third of all marine life perishes.

Third Trumpet Sounds:
(Revelation 8:10-11)

The Third Trumpet Sounds. This Trumpet Judgment is similar to the Second Trumpet Judgment; the difference is it contaminates freshwater lakes and rivers of the planet rather than the oceans. The Apostle John sees this Judgment as a Great Star descending from heaven blazing like a torch, and it poisons one-third of the available water supply. Many people die as a result of this poisoned water supply. A name, Wormwood, is given to this Star. It is called Artemisia Absinthium (scientifically speaking) which is known as a shrub plant that is notorious for the intense bitterness and deadly qualities it possesses.

Fourth Trumpet Sounds:
(Revelation 8:12-13)

In this Judgment, John observes that the sun, moon, and a third of the stars are all struck so that a third are darkened. He then proclaims he sees another angel fly through the sky, announcing more "woes" to Earth's inhabitants and that they will undergo more severe Judgments with the following three Trumpet blasts.

Fifth Trumpet Sound:
(Revelation 9:1-12)

John the Apostle is shown an angel descending from Heaven with a key. God instructs this angel to open the "bottomless pit." Out of this pit, demonic beings that look like a locust are released and have tails that sting; the sting is like a scorpion sting. The pain is so great that people will seek suicide, and death will flee four-five months, scripture tells us. The angel restricts the demonic locust creatures from hurting any green grass and trees and only hurting those who do not have the seal of God, which are the 144,000 Jewish Evangelists and other new converts.

Sixth Trumpet Sounds:
(Revelation 9:13-19)

Following the Fifth Trumpet Judgment, God sends this next angel to release four fallen angels bound in the Great Euphrates River. God has held them there for this specific time. It is the "Second Woe" upon the Earth. The four fallen angels command a legion of two hundred million mounted troops; the horses are seen as spewing brimstone, fire, and smoke from their mouths. Before the hostilities are unleashed at the Great Euphrates River, the Sixth Angel sounds the Trumpet. The Middle Eastern countries of Syria, Iraq, Turkey, and Iran are all connected by a canal at the Euphrates River.

China's population of over one-billion people means it can deploy an army of 200 million soldiers and a coalition of Islamic countries to muster an equal force. When the Antichrist World leader establishes his Final World Empire, which is imminent, a significant conflict will break out in the Middle East and usher in what the ancient text has always proven to be correct, the Abomination of Desolation spoken of by Daniel the prophet, during the Great Tribulation.

Other events follow the Sixth Trumpet sound:

John is instructed to prophesy what he sees as the angel leads him. **(Revelation 10:8-11).**

The angel also announces that the "Times of the Gentiles" will end in forty-two months (3.5 years)

Two Witnesses Dressed in Sackcloth Appear:

At this time, the Two Witnesses come on the scene dressed in sackcloth and prophesy in the streets of Jerusalem for 3.5 years. "They have the power to close heaven, so it doesn't rain for three-and-one-half years, and convert all waters to blood, and strike the Earth with many plagues, as often as the desire." **(Revelation 11:6).**

Seventh Trumpet Sounds:

(Revelation 11:15-18)

Rejoicing in Heaven:

Next, John hears great voices in Heaven announcing the end of all things is come on Earth, and the Lord Jesus will establish His

Kingdom on Earth to last One Thousand Years. Great rejoicing is now in Heaven, and everyone worships the King in all His glory with adoration and praise to Jesus.

Great Wrath on Earth

As much happiness and joy occur in Heaven, God's judgments continue to fall on Earth. Sadly though, those who have survived all the plagues, earthquakes, and horrors on Earth continue to curse God because of those plagues and refuse to repent of their sins and iniquities.

The scriptures tell us great hail and more earthquakes continue. **(Revelation 11:19).**

War Breaks Out in the Spiritual Realm:

During this time, a great battle breaks out in the spiritual realm. Michael, the archangel, is instructed by God to cast the Red Dragon (Satan) to Earth. Satan no longer has access to the throne of God to accuse God's people. Michael, the archangel, does what he was commanded, and Satan is then cast to the Earth with great wrath because he knows he has little time left.

Satan is Angry and Attacks the Jewish People:

Now that the devil can no longer accuse God's people and is cast down to earth, he begins his attacks on the Jewish people in Israel. War breaks out in the Middle East, and Israel's haters start their assaults on the nation of Israel.

The Time of Jacobs's Trouble

Israel has always suffered from her surrounding enemies, but now it begins to intensify. However, there is hope for the Jewish people because God always protects His own. As mentioned, he has prepared a hiding place for them in the Rose colored Caves of "Petra," an ancient city in the Jordan wilderness. **(Revelation 12: 1-17).**

21

The Antichrist & Mid-Tribulation

(Revelation 13)

Midway through the Tribulation, the Antichrist breaks his covenant with the Jewish people in Israel. The Jewish people whom this evil World leader deceived now realize what is at stake, and the Beast leader is not really who they thought he was.

The "Abomination of Desolation" is set up by the False Prophet in the newly built Temple in Jerusalem. It is an image of the Beast which can talk (AI) and causes all Earth's inhabitants to receive the "mark" (666) on their Right Hand or Forehead.

During this time, the World dictator is satanically possessed, and he sits in the temple and proclaims to be God. Remember, Satan and his demonic minions are already kicked out of the heavens and are now walking the Earth.

Satan takes up residence in the World leader, as he becomes so powerful in his evil schemes deceiving millions to take his "mark."

He punishes the Jewish people and others who commit to Jesus, and he has extreme hatred toward them because Jesus has defeated him; he knows he only has 3.5 years to deceive humanity to receive the "mark."

In (Revelation 13: 5-7) tells us Satan begins his cursing toward the Highest and those in Heaven, and he is given the freedom to do this for 3.5 years; his hate grows more intense toward the Jewish people and others who commit to Jesus as he slaughters millions.

The Antichrist army goes on a rampage to round up all who refuse the "mark."

At this current time, future supporters of the coming World leader are setting in motion the system for all the World to receive the "mark."

Digital currency is how they will track everyone on Earth. In (Revelation 13:16-18) the scriptures are pretty straightforward: "No one is allowed to buy or sell without that mark."

The "Digital currency" that is implemented is for this reason. It is why two Senators introduced a bill to be put in place for everyone to receive a "Digital I.D."

They need the digital I.D. to have the digital currency.

Under the Beast regime, you must show the "mark" with all your information if you want to eat. The cashier will scan your "mark" at the grocery counter during cash out. It applies to buying gas for your car, medicines, and everything else a person needs to survive.

Imagine living in a world where humanity is branded as cattle and living under a totalitarian One World Government.

As bad as conditions were for the Jewish people under Hitler, living under the Satanic Antichrist regime would be much worse.

I cannot stress enough that everything unfolding on the World stage is for ushering in that Final World Empire ruled by the Beast, Antichrist.

The transformation of our country and the rules and laws put into place are all for that specific reason.

The World is moving quickly to fulfill all Prophecy has declared concerning the Return of the Lord Jesus Christ.

Before all this, though, God declares He will destroy the world's evil, which is why His Judgments will fall when He pours out His Wrath upon all those whose names are not written in the "Book of Life" during the last seven years of the Tribulation, under the Final World Empire the prophet Daniel spoke about.

The Apostle John is Shown More Visions:
(Revelation 14:1-5)

Now, John sees the 144,000 Jewish Evangelists standing on Mt. Zion with Jesus, and they have the seal of God on their foreheads. They will begin their evangelism to those who are searching for the truth.

(Revelation 14:6-7) Another angel is seen flying through mid-heaven (Universe), proclaiming the message of Salvation to those that dwell upon Earth one last time. He is giving a fare-warning to fear God and give glory to Him because the End of all things is here.

(Revelation 14:8) Next, an angel appears, proclaiming Babylon is fallen. The Book of Revelation mentions two Babylons: Political Babylon and Ecclesiastical Babylon. The angel here refers to Political Babylon, where the Antichrist will establish his headquarters, and Rome is the city the angel talks about.

Some prophecy teachers believe the Antichrist will take up residence in N.Y. city because the UN is there, and they will be critical players in backing the Beast regime. I don't believe that version and will prove this to you in a later chapter.

(Revelation 14:9-12) Now comes another angel proclaiming with a loud voice, "If anyone worships the Beast and his image and takes his "mark" on their right hand or forehead, they shall receive the "full wrath" of God poured out." He continues to pronounce that those that do this will be tormented with fire and brimstone in the presence of the Lamb (Jesus) and His holy angels.

Earth dwellers that take the "mark" will be thrown into the fire-and-brimstone lake, and such individuals will not be shown any mercy.

Here is the "fare-warning" for anyone who decides to take that "mark," as I just gave you the words Jesus spoke to His holy angel to proclaim to those who will have to make that choice soon.

It is best to receive Jesus Christ now and "repent" your sins while there is still time. Those who become new believers during the horrific Tribulation will be rounded up and sent to the camps for re-education (brainwashed) into accepting the "mark" of the Beast.

If you reject the "mark, you will be executed by beheading, most likely in the camps.

The scriptures tell us that millions will be slaughtered for faith in Jesus because they refuse the "mark," but when that happens, they will immediately be in the Lord's presence and those who have arrived before them.

As the above scripture is self-explanatory, those who take the "mark" will prolong their life by 3.5 years and immediately banish into everlasting torment in the Lake of Fire with Satan, the Beast, and the False Prophet.

It is best to be ready now and allow Jesus to transform your life so that you will be spared from what is coming when the rapture occurs. No one knows when the Lord returns because He said, "I will come as a thief in the night, so be ready."

Living under the Final World Empire would be unimaginable. Knowing what is to come and the horror, it would be unbelievable not to make the right decision.

The ruling – class believes they have reached perfection, and the New World system they are working so feverishly to establish in the next few years will be something they least expect.

It is best to remember that the Prophecy will come to pass. Whether you believe this or not doesn't matter; if God proclaims something, that is, end of story! So Be Ready!

Battle of Armageddon
(Revelation 14: 14-20)

The Apostle is next shown a prelude to the Battle of Armageddon that will occur at the end of the Tribulation, living under the Final World Empire.

So many will die in this battle that the ancient texts tell us the blood of those killed will reach a Horse's bridle, and it is described as running One Thousand Six Hundred Furlongs, which is 200 miles. We will explore more on the Battle of Armageddon in a later chapter.

A Glorious Heavenly Scene
(Revelation 15: 1-4)

John describes a great scene taking place in Heaven. He describes a "sea of transparent glass" and seeing all those who did not receive the Beast mark of his number (666) or name. These believers are standing on the "sea of glass" with gold harps in their hands and singing a new song, the song of Moses.

He then sees another magnificent event. Heaven's Temple of the Tabernacle of the Testimony is opened:

Seven angels emerge with the last plagues from the Temple, clothed in pure white linen and a golden Sachs on their robes. These angels are given "vials" full of the Wrath of God.

The Temple in Heaven is seen as being filled with smoke from the glory of God after the last Seven angels come out holding the final plagues of God in their "vials." The scripture tells us no one could enter the Temple in Heaven until the Seven angels pour out their "vials" filled with the Wrath of God upon the Earth.

22

Seven Vials" Poured Upon Earth

"First Vial Judgment
(Revelation 16:1-2)

Oozing and stinking sores (like boils) break out over the people who have the Beast mark and worship his statue as a result of the "first vial" judgment poured out by the angel.

This plague will strike those who have chosen to follow the Anti-christ World leader; the faithful followers of Jesus Christ during the Tribulation in the Final World Empire will be spared from this plague.

"Second Vial Judgment"
(Revelation 16:3)

The second angel released the contents of his vial into the Sea, and the water was turned into blood like a dead man (probably almost black). The "Second Trumpet" judgment fell upon 1/3 of the Sea. This "vial" judgment is poured out on what is left of the Sea. One-third of the marine life perished during the Second Trumpet; now, anything left of the marine life is gone. The oceans are no longer oceans, and they are dead.

"Third Vial Judgment"
(Revelation 16:4-7)

The rivers and freshwater springs that the Third Trumpet Judgment contaminated one-third of the World's rivers and lakes have now become blood. The angel that pours out this plague declares; You are righteous, O Lord, for your Judgment, for they've shed your saints and prophets' blood, and you have given them blood to drink, and they are worthy of this.

"Fourth Vial Judgment"
(Revelation16:8-9)

The "Fourth vial," like the "Fourth Trumpet," impacts the heavenly bodies, in this case, the sun. The Fourth Trumpet will affect a third of the sun, moon, and stars, causing a third of the day and night to be eclipsed in darkness.

In contrast, the "Fourth Vial" Judgment only affects the sun, and its contents cause earth **inhabitants to be burnt by fire since the sun's strength is increased.**

Even while earth dwellers know that the plagues originate from God, they continue to reject them; this severe judgment inflicted onto the planet does not bring humanity to "repent" but only intensifies their cursing toward the "Highest."

"Fifth Vial Judgment"
(Revelation 16:10-11)

The headquarters of the Satanic World leader and his regime and supporters are the targets of the "Fifth Vial" Judgment. Darkness, anguish, and the combined impact of the previous judgment with oozing and stinking sores inflicted from the "First Vial" Judgment on all those that took the "mark" of the Beast now are causing tremendous suffering.

The "Fifth Vial" Judgment causes great darkness across the globe.

Such darkness equals the "ninth plague" in Egypt under Moses (Exodus 10:21-23), and because those who took the "mark" feel such incredible pain from the sores inflicted upon them, still, they continue to curse God.

"Sixth Vial Judgment"
(Revelation 16: 12-16)

The Great Euphrates River is completely dried up due to the Sixth Angel as his "vial" is poured upon it, creating a road for the Kings (leaders) coming from the east.

These eastern Kings' military branches have arrived and will fight against the Beast and the invasion of Israel.

Three unclean spirits emerge from the dragon (Satan), Antichrist, and the False Prophet during this time. The Bible tells us they have the power to do miracles and summon all the Kings (world leaders) of the earth to the battle of the great day.

The battle refers to "The Battle of Armageddon. It is the specified area where Jesus will descend from Heaven to Earth in all splendor and majesty to slay the armies of the Beast and the False Prophet as they attack Israel. It will also consist of the remaining 200 million military troops from the Far East and others.

This military conflict fulfills Daniel 2:35's prophecy about the "Smiting Stone." Jesus is the smiting stone Daniel is referring to.

"Seventh Vial Judgment"
(Revelation 16:17-21)

An angel in the air pours out this final "vial judgment, and Great voices are heard coming from the Temple in Heaven out of the throne, proclaiming, "It is done."

The largest Earthquake ever in the history of the world is now taking place. So Great an earthquake that it splits Babylon (Rome) into three different sections.

It is so massive that every city crumbles to the ground, and every mountain on earth falls; the islands no longer exist because they, too, have vanished.

The fierceness of God's Wrath is now felt all over the world.

It is destruction for all those whose names are not written in the Book of Life.

One more terrifying event takes place under this "Seventh Vial" Judgment.

Massive hail begins to fall from Heaven on all Earth's inhabitants, those whose names are not in the Book of Life.

The ancient manuscripts tell us that the Hailstone weighs a "talent," equal to a one-hundred-pound hailstone.

The Antichrist supporters continue to curse God, the "texts" tells us, because of those plagues falling to earth.

Just imagine one-hundred-pound hailstones falling from the sky! Do you want to be here to experience all these plagues?

These "horrors" are predicted to occur, and Jesus Himself tells us this.

The Final World Empire predicted by the prophets and Jesus will undoubtedly be fulfilled as Narcissism is Rising, as the ancient texts tell us will occur because, at this current time, narcissistic individuals have an Antichrist spirit working in them to establish their Final One-World Tower of Babel.

We have explored through the chapters all the "Judgments" that will occur under the Final World Empire regime.

More events follow!

23

Mystery Babylon

(Revelation 17:1-13)

Living under the Final World Empire, Earth's inhabitants must conform to a problematic and unimaginable reality; "Survival" is the fitting word!

The Apostle John is shown another "Wonder" in Heaven, and he sees a woman sitting on a scarlet-colored beast, and this woman is referred to as the Harlot, Mystery Babylon. (Rev17:5).

"Mystery Babylon" represents "Ecclesiastical Babylon" (Apostate Christianity).

The Scarlet-colored beast, the woman, sits on represents "Political Babylon."

There is a union between the two. Where one goes, the other goes.

The Harlot's clothing colors are purple and scarlet, decked with precious gems, gold, and silver.

She is holding a golden cup in her hand, full of cursing and filthiness and drunken with the blood of the righteous and those who have given their lives for Jesus (Revelation 17:4-6).

The Harlot (apostate church) powers the Fourth and Final World Empires.

The Scarlet Beast she rides, Political Babylon, is the Antichrist's confederated empire, the last form of Gentile World Dominion.

The Scarlet-colored Beast has seven heads and ten horns. The Seven heads represent seven kings, and the ten horns are the ten world regions we discussed in a previous chapter. These ten regions will have a leader (king) over each area, and they will give all their power and support to the Satanic world leader, the Antichrist.

The "Apostate church," Mystery Babylon, is believed by many Prophecy scholars to embrace all world religions and will form the "One World Religion" during the Final World Empire.

Rome is the location of "Mystery Babylon," leading many to believe it is the Vatican.

This present Pope is a strong proponent of uniting all the world's religions, as he has been instrumental in announcing this.

The description the Apostle John records in the Book of Revelation of the Harlot dressed in colors of Scarlet and Purple are colorings of the minister's garments of a mainline denomination in the world with a golden cup the Harlot is holding is used during their services.

John's description says the women (apostate church) are drunk with the blood of Jesus' martyrs and saints.

If you have not read "Foxes Book of Martyrs," I encourage you to do so. It records the massive persecution, especially during the 15th& 16th centuries, of Christians by the papal, and many were burned at the stake and accused of being witches involved in sorcery. They did not renounce their faith in Jesus but chose to die for His namesake.

An ecclesiastical tribunal was formed in 1232 by Pope Gregory 1X to end heresy, and its activities were primarily concentrated in southern France and northern Italy and gained a notorious reputation for its use of torture.

Re-established in 1542 to combat Prostastism, the papal inquisition eventually became an organ of papal governance.

The Spanish Inquisition was an ecclesiastical court founded in Roman Catholic Spain in 1478, initially to prosecute converts to Judaism and Islam, but later to charge Prostastism. It was ruthless in terms of torture and execution.

John the Apostle writes more about what he sees as he is instructed to do so by the angel.

(Rev 17:15-18) Show that the Confederated Empire of the Narcissistic World leader, the Beast, comprised of the Ten Kings over the Ten regional areas, will hate the Harlot (world church) and eventually destroy her by fire because God will allow it.

Mystery Babylon will be destroyed because God's Word is true and will be fulfilled.

(Rev 17:16) Tell us in "one hour," the "Apostate church" is destroyed, and the entire city is burned to the ground. Not many want to believe it; unfortunately, it is Prophecy and will come to pass.

Feel free to research this; I have given you the scripture verses.

(Rev 18) Reveal how the merchants of the earth "wail" over the loss of this mighty city (Rome). They were made rich through all their greed and power. The merchants described are the current, significant corporations of this era.

They are aligning under the new transformation of our world system, as instructed, to be under the umbrella of the Global economy when it becomes fully established, at the latest, (2030), if not sooner.

Research (Revelation 18) tells how Economic Babylon, the Global economy of the Confederated Empire of the Beast, is destroyed when the Apostate Church is removed.

As the verses tell us, during the destruction of that "Great City," those that trade by the sea and all other merchants will be terrified because all the global wealth they thought would last forever, in one hour, was obliterated.

The Final World Empire is the beginning of the end of all things as earth dwellers will be caught in the "snare" (trap) they set for themselves because they rejected the truth of how to be spared from all the cataclysmic events that fall upon them.

24

A World View, Narcissism

Everyone has a worldview on different things and bases their everyday decisions on those worldviews.

Your worldview stems from who you are and contributes to your character.

Christians are supposed to hold to a Biblical worldview, some still do, but most no longer have.

There are two groups of people in the world. —those with a Biblical worldview and those without.

Those without a Biblical worldview lack a moral compass to guide their decision-making through life and are one form or another, narcissists.

Narcissism is a spiritual problem; they lack correct decision-making. Without a Biblical worldview, they lack a strong foundation on which to stand, so all without the correct worldview have narcissist traits, which is insanity.

To better understand, Narcissism is a sin, a word we no longer hear in the pagan age we live in.

Born Again believers no longer practice those narcissistic traits and now have a different Biblical perspective.

There are many forms of narcissism, some are soft narcissists, and others are hard-core, contributing to their worldview choices.

Belief in God and religious practices have declined dramatically in America and worldwide, and only 44% of Christians believe Jesus lead a sinless life. What is the cause of this? Narcissism is Rising!

When you cast God out of your life, you lack structure in sound decision-making.

Within the past few years, society has taken a nosedive, morally speaking, and as a result, negativity now rules.

A narcissistic worldview is the perfect example of humanity that will enter The Final World Empire. Why do I say this? Because we are already witnessing madness in some areas of the world and are half-way through the Great Reset of this World system.

Try to imagine living under a regime that does not have to give an account for the bad choices made by ordinary people. I don't believe it is hard to imagine this; we have witnessed it in one form or another for some time now.

Living under "The Final World Empire" will be living under a dangerously dark worldview.

Narcissists do not feel they have to give account to anyone despite how wrong their choices are.

Looking back, some recent choices made by some officials show nothing more than overwhelming arrogance and harmful decisions, yet, the masses must conform.

America and the world's future are grim and painfully sad : **(Proverbs 29:2,4). "When good people prosper, society benefits; when evil people rule, everyone moans.**

(4) By justice, a King gives a nation stability, but those greedy for bribes tear it down."

Global events plaguing our planet for the past few years have brought about rapid change by accelerating the predicted Final World Empire.

It is clear the worldview some officials are taking, and it puts to question what they are working toward.

A person can never rise above their worldview; it decides their destiny. Please pay close attention to the worldview of others, especially those in power, because it reveals their intentions for society.

Understanding someone's worldview will help you distinguish if they have your best interest.

Now more than ever, it is imperative that you are not deceived because Jesus told us deception would be everywhere in this generation, just as in the Days of Noah and Lot.

25

A Society Based on Lies

We no longer are a society based on truth; what we witness daily is anything but the truth.

Narcissism is Rising! Truth is not accepted.

Promoters of The Final World Government suggest, in many ways, that reality is no longer needed, and the narrative they present is all that is required.

Those holding a Biblical worldview are considered outdated and ignorant in their logic.

The coming Final World Empire (agenda 2030) will not allow truth-bearers in their new civilization.

Wealthy World leaders have already set the precedent of what is welcomed in their Utopia. The "new world" promoters have a different mindset than the average citizen.

Their script is not based on truth; the lie is what matters. It is very plain if you are intuned to "watching" as Jesus warned His people to do so they won't be deceived.

Tricky and dangerous times are coming; actually, they are here now but will get much worse.

It is essential to understand what comes with living under the predicted World government, the globalist Utopia of Agenda 2030.

Sadly, America is no longer made up of serious people. The lie is the point, and that's how it is.

I am grateful though, that there still is a small minority of people that hold to a Biblical worldview. As mentioned, anything other than that is nothing more than insanity.

A Biblical worldview is true. Not accepting the fact is accepting deceit.

We are now a society based on deceit. Did you ask why? Just look around at some recent issues presented to the public.

Can you honestly say everything looks the same and things are every day? Some would argue that what is normal to one is not customary to another. I guess that is true only partly, but to the one who does not recognize normal, insanity rules them. Yes, and I did say that!

Hopefully, you understand the point I am trying to present.

Without a Biblical worldview, the only thing left is deceit, so we are now a country based on deception. Once again, if God is tossed out, which He is, as that is the choice of most, here we are!

Because deceit now rules, it is essential (for those with eyes to see and ears to hear) to plan accordingly.

As mentioned, when the "Lie is upheld," and Truth is banished, only insanity remains, and this is precisely what the masses are being forced to accept.

A false reality is being presented to humanity, and living conditions under the coming new civilization under the Final World Empire will be anything but ordinary.

It is imperative to understand the culture at this time is forced to accept an ideology based on lies and deceit.

Many of the ruling class followed Sal Alinsky, and he wrote the book, “Rules for Radicals.” It’s based on the communist manifesto.

The ideology that is now in progress is based on everything that opposes God, Truth, and Reality.

As mentioned, a whole generation is “groomed” into an ideology that opposes Truth.

It is why we are now witnessing and forced to embrace crazy, abnormal beliefs and characteristics that some species live by.

There is no resistance to the ideology forced upon the populace.

Earth-dwellers are forced to accept the ideology based on lies and fraud.

Unfortunately, some hard-core narcissists are in control of leading humanity to their ultimate demise. When Truth vanished, deceit filled the void.

Narcissism is Rising! We are only seeing the beginning stages of what will come under this New World Regime, with psychopaths and sociopaths in control, under the leadership of the demonic himself, the Antichrist.

God the Father and Jesus are Truth (Psalm 31:5, John 14:6).

Satan is a liar.

A nation that decides to give up truth and become one of deceit, fraud, and deception chooses to transform into one that is an obscenity to God.

A nation established in the Bible cannot decide to turn its back on God and then choose to follow Satan without having dire consequences thrust upon that nation.

Bible History shows precisely what the results of a country were left once they chose to ignore the Rules and laws of God and nature.

I have studied the ancient text, and honestly, with my observations, I cannot understand why God has not already poured out His Wrath.

In His mercy, He still is giving more time for those last chosen few on earth to commit to Jesus, and get their name written in the

Book of Life, then the "fullness of the gentiles" will be complete, and the terrifying events foretold about the Tribulation period will commence.

In the meantime, deceit and fraud are taking over the masses.

In Boston, Mass, "SatanCon," a group of Satan worshippers met for their second annual meeting and doubled in size from their first secession. After-school care Sation clubs are springing up all over the nation.

The Final World Empire's Goals are the 2030 Sustainable Development Goals, passed into law on January 1, 2016.

Here is a summary of their goals:

- **They are anti-Christian and aim to convert the world's population into an anti-God belief system.**
- **Their goal is to create a global regime that is neither elected nor democratic.**
- **To have a government instruct on parenting and education, parents must obey.**
- **To force their ideology and values on every individual on earth.**
- **Under the Final World Empire (2030 Agenda), a new civilization will emerge, and everyone will act accordingly to the rules or face harsh consequences.**

Two US Senators introduced legislation (Senate Bill 884) to create a digital identity for every U.S. citizen. Eight days later, it passed with a favorable recommendation from the appropriate Senate committee.

A digital ID will enable the tracking of all individuals, and it can control a person's bank account, medical records, driver's license, Social Security number, etc.

One of those Senators that introduced the bill attended the

Bilderberg meeting of 2022 and the World Economic Forum meeting of 2023.

As you can see, the establishment of the Final World Empire (2030 Agenda) is well on its way.

A society based on lies and fraud to control all of humanity is not a conspiracy theory but is very real and, indeed, a truthful fact.

Everything is out in the open; the globalists tell us directly what they are doing as they build their new civilization, their Tower of Babel.

Earth's inhabitants will live under a new civilization based on lies and fraud.

As we progress toward this dark regime, leaders worldwide are changing the rules and laws to fit their ideology for all earth dwellers.

As a country, we have chosen to ignore the Truth and choose the Lie instead.

Truth has vanished, and deceit is welcomed.

It is a perfect environment for proponents of a one-world government to welcome their coming leader, the Antichrist, under the Final World Empire.

26

The Marriage Supper & Second Coming

(Revelation 19:1-21)

Just after Mystery Babylon is destroyed, a grand celebration occurs in Heaven, as John the Apostle writes; and hearing voices honoring God for His righteous judgments of the Harlot (apostate church) on earth; declaring, genuine and honest are those judgments because of the blood spilled of the saints and martyrs of Jesus.

The Marriage Supper

Next, an event occurs that all true believers in Jesus have anxiously awaited to arrive. It is the glorious event, the Marriage Supper of the Lamb.

This Grand event is the consummation of Jesus Christ and the True Church as His bride. (Revelation 19:7-9). Those that attend this glorious event will be clothed in fine linen, clean and white. This fine linen represents the righteousness of all those who have been faithful to Jesus on earth, despite the intense suffering, trials, and tests they have encountered from those who are haters of God and His people.

During this time, "rewards" will be given to the faithful followers of the Lamb in Heaven.

At the Marriage Supper of the Lamb, countless millions worldwide will attend this Glorious Wedding Feast known as the Marriage Supper of the Lamb, along with the Lamb of God, Jesus our Savior.

This celebration occurs when the entire church, also known as (the bride), is united with the Lord Jesus, the bridegroom.

The Marriage Supper occurs in Heaven at the end of the Tribulation; while much suffering happens on earth, rejoicing occurs in Heaven.

The Second Coming & Armageddon

Under the Final World Empire, the greatest war in civilization's history will occur.

World War One and Two, as bad as it was, and the loss of life cannot compare to the Battle of Armageddon that will commence at the end of the Tribulation under the Final World Empire.

First and foremost, one must consider the culture during this time and the military armies fighting in this war. The Antichrist world leader will lead his military into the valley of *"Megiddo"* to invade Israel in hopes of eradicating that tiny country.

(Revelation 16:13-14,16) Tell us demonic entities from Satan, The Beast, and the False Prophet will go forth and summon the earth's kings and their armies to fight in this war.

The kings over the Ten regions that support the Beast will gather their armies to fight.

All those taking part in this great catastrophe under each regional king will have taken the "mark" of the beast. They are all narcissistic Reprobates belonging to Satan now.

The "culture mindset" of those taking part in the Battle of Armageddon think they can exterminate the Jewish race and prevent the

Lord Jesus from Returning to earth; Satan believes he can win a war with the Messiah, Jesus Christ.

The 200 million-man armies of the Kings of the east also gather to fight in this war.

As mentioned, this battle will be so great that the bloodshed will reach a horse's bridle and run for two hundred miles, the ancient texts say.

The Fowls Great Feast
(Revelation 19:17-18)

At this time, the angel is instructed to "call" all the fowls that fly in mid-heaven to this great feast God has prepared for them; they will eat the flesh and the horses of those fighting in this Battle.

God's fury will come up in His face when the armies under the Final World Empire, led by the evil World leader, prepare to battle against God's people, the Jewish race.

Jesus Returns to Earth
(Revelation 19:17-19)

The Apostle John sees a spectacular event next: Heaven opens, and a White Horse is seen with Jesus Christ, who is King of King and Lord of Lords, riding the white horse with all of Heaven's armies (faithful followers of Christ), following Him on White Horses clothed in fine linen, clean and white.

It is the "Second Coming" of Christ taking place, but first, Jesus takes care of his remaining enemies and those fighting against Israel.

The scriptures tell us that the False Prophet and the Beast are thrust into a burning lake of fire and brimstone by Jesus, and the remnant in the armies was slain by Him who sat upon the white horse.

Satan Bound for 1,000 Years
(Revelation 20:1-3)

A strong angel is next seen having the "key" to the bottomless pit, and John makes mention of this strong angel having a chain in his hand.

The angel then grabs the dragon (Satan), casts him into the bottomless pit, and puts a "seal" on him.

The evil serpent, the devil, is cast into that "pit" for 1,000 years. He will be released after a thousand years to "tempt" humanity again; it will not last long, however, as the Bible explains, God the Father will strike him and throw him into a lake of fire for a thousand years, along with all those who don't have their name written in the Book of Life.

The Kingdom Age

The earth is cleansed after the Battle of Armageddon, and the Kingdom Age begins.

It is a time of universal peace, prosperity, and joy, long life for those born during this time, and free from Satan's oppression of sickness, heartaches, murders, human trafficking, drug dealing, gangs, wars, violence, exploitation of children, and harm to them; and so much more is gone.

During the Kingdom Age, Satan will be tossed into the abyss for one thousand years.

Jesus will rule the earth and be King over it.

We will have plenty of time to talk with the Lord and ask Him questions, primarily to praise and worship Him.

Meeting loved ones and the saints of all ages, along with the Apostles who were the first to spread the good news, the gospel of Jesus Christ, after He was crucified and ascended to Heaven.

The ancient texts tell us even the animal kingdom will be at peace. The lamb and lion will graze together.

All the earth will be at rest and enjoy living in harmony with our Savior, the Lord Jesus Christ.

27

More Things That Will Take Place

We have just explored some of those main events, the 21 judgments, and other situations that will take place under the Final World Empire.

The Book of Revelation explains the reality concerning the Revelation of Jesus Christ and His Return at the end of the Seven-Year Tribulation.

(Revelation1:1-2) It is the beginning of the Book of Revelation. It tells us that everything written in the "book" God sent and signified those things written by His angel to the Apostle John, those things that "Will" surely come to pass.

The "Book" Presents:

- An inventory of items is presented to God's people, so they will understand the signs coming to pass.
- A compilation of events that "Will" occur.

- A collection of "conditions" that "Will" be met despite humanity's negative opinions or ignorance on the subject matter.
- A record of events; 21 Judgments, Mystery Babylon, the Two Witness dressed in sackcloth, the Marriage Supper, etc., revealed to the Apostle John.
- The "Prophetic Word of God" is The Book of Revelation.
- Jesus Christ is that Book's "Witness" and His "Testimony."

Under the Final World Empire, These Events "Will" Occur:

First and foremost, There "Will" be a Final World Empire of Control and Power.

(Revelation 13:7) Is self-explanatory about a Malignant Narcissistic World leader, the Beast, who is given power, great authority, and control over all the world's nations.

It is without question, or any doubt, the verse refers to "Agenda 2030," "The Great Reset," and "The Final World Empire" predicted by the prophets and Jesus Himself.

Mystery Babylon A Global Religion "Will" Emerge:

(Revelation 13:8) Gives "clarity" on the subject, the global religion of all those who do not have their name written in The Book of Life, those who have taken the "mark of the Beast" inscribed on their right hand or forehead will "worship" the Antichrist Beast, and his image of Revelation 13:8.

The scripture tells us that all those who dwell on the earth shall worship the Lawless one,

And their names are not recorded in the Lambs Book.

World Religion starts with the combined religions of the world into one (probably under one of the most prominent mainline denominations). Still, it is later destroyed by the Beast because he wants to be the one object of worship. It is after the combined religions of the world are destroyed, and the Beast sits in the newly built temple demanding worship from all humanity. They pledge allegiance to him by taking his "mark."

Remember, the "mark" is the devil's "mark," and those who take it will be thrown into the Lake of Fire and Brimstone.

Under the leadership of the Beast, all derogatory acts individuals commit, and practice will be a branch of the "worship" of the Beast because he is the persona of evil, himself being possessed by Satan.

It indicates the trajectory of the unbiblical ethic circulating the globe of a newly founded branch of religion that almost all humanity, including a large portion of the church, now accepts.

The "Trans" movement and woke are the new branches of a new religion in the country.

Elites demand that everyone embrace this newly founded religion. You "must" love and accept it.

It requires those still faithful to biblical views to renounce their beliefs and accept their new religious system.

However, there is one significant and primary issue here; to reject that "sin" does not exist means Jesus is unnecessary.

It is that simple, and this is why under the Beast regime, all true believers in Jesus Christ, those that refuse the "mark" will have one final opportunity to get the "mark" or be executed by beheading according to **(Revelation 20:4).**

If you "doubt" this, please at least take the time to look up the verse for yourself.

The Antichrist spirit is already at work currently in this country and world. It is why we witness the madness unleashed in every facet of our society, without any hindrance or secrets but out in the open and displayed to the public. We can see that the Beast regime is under construction and nearly complete.

The supporters of the Great Reset, Final World Empire, are actively doing what they do best because their soon-coming world leaders' "spirit" has summoned them to continue in a reprobate mindset by supporting all the unbiblical ethics society offers.

The "world stage" is almost complete for their beloved leader to appear, and the masses will all run like "herded cattle" to be "branded" by the "mark" of their Satanic Beast.

Under the Final World Empire, the earth's inhabitants will worship Satan, the enemy of creation.

We have already witnessed the "lovers of darkness" shaking their fits in God's face. They "hate" God, and if you are still "true" to the faith, they "hate" you also.

As mentioned, they do not want to share the planet with you.

The "reality" of this whole situation; is that if you are still a follower of Jesus Christ and have not "caved" to the "unbiblical ethic" of the world, you may not be comfortable around them as well.

It works just that way! You are an individual who has a "right" to make your own choice of who and what you "worship."

Stay strong in the faith, take your stand with God's followers, and don't "cave" to the demands of the ungodly who prefer darkness over light.

Jesus said the generation that sees all these things happening is the generation that witnesses His Return.

Sadly, those still part of the "faithful remnant" are outnumbered. The Earth dwellers of the coming Final World Empire are revealing who they "worship," and it is not the God we serve.

As mentioned, everything is out in the "open" now; and we see who is faithful to God and Jesus and those that "Hate" God and His followers.

There will be Global Depopulation.

(Revelation 13:15) Tells us that the False Prophet has the power to give life to the statue of the Antichrist, and it will be able to talk and cause anyone who does not take the mark and worship the image to be executed.

As mentioned, this is artificial intelligence (Al)—a computerized talking statue.

A Planetary Marking System

(Revelation 13:16) Describe that everyone on the Globe is required to receive the imprint (mark) of the Beast.

There definitely "Will" be a Global Marking system that distinguishes (IDs), the supporters of the Final World Empire, and those who refuse the marking system.

The authorities will likely use hand scanning and facial recognition to keep control over humanity.

Economic Global System

(Revelation 13:17) Tell us, without a "mark," the public cannot buy or sell. To purchase necessities for daily living, you need an (ID), a "Mark."

The government compels everyone under the Final World Empire to purchase and sell.

The aim is to replace cash with digital currency.

The Return of Jesus Christ

Jesus was talking to His disciples, and they asked Him to tell them of the "signs" of His Return and the End of the Age.

He explained to them that the generation that sees (Revelation 13) coming to pass, and other signs, would be the generation that sees His Return.

(Matthew 24) Tell us the world will be as the Days of Noah and Lot when the End comes.

Our generation is seeing all those "signs" coming to pass, and we are watching (Revelation 13) the establishment of Beasts Regime, the Final World Empire nearing completion.

Unsurprisingly, we see almost everything mentioned in this chapter happening.

28

The Great Invasion

Now, we are witnesses to an invasion taking place at our country's southern border.

Tens of thousands of undocumented immigrants are pouring into our country every day.

Most Americans are oblivious to the full gravity of this invasion's implications.

This invasion is taking place because it significantly contributes to those "Resetting" the country.

The slogan, "Great Reset," is why it is happening. They were being "truthful" when they first introduced that term to you, and what is happening is out in the open now.

A List of Why They Need Open Borders

- It aids in the "dismantling" of the country by breaking down the economy. Taxpayers are funding the plan to service and meet all the needs of each immigrant entering America. They take priority over American citizens, and homeless Vets have been kicked out of shelters so immigrants can have their spot.

- The plan is to create tension to fuel the fires of radicals so that anarchy and chaos will start, aiding the globalists to come in with a solution; in the end, Martial Law, so the country goes into lockdown and control of the masses.
- The World Economic Forum's slogan, "Being Happy Owning Nothing." Klaus Schwab's dream is coming to pass! Currently, the immigrants own nothing and are happy they are being cared for; by you, the American citizen. Too bad, however, Klaus Schwab didn't complete the story when he first announced how happy everyone would be not owning anything; oh, maybe, just maybe, it slipped his mind not telling you, you are the one who will be funding their plan at taxpayer expense?
- They are turning the country into a vast welfare state through your generous contributions to funding their goals; it is part of the plan written in the "Communist Manifesto" about "distributing the wealth." Wealthy countries will support the less fortunate countries, and it is precisely what they are doing.

Nothing wrong, of course, with helping others, but it will not end that way because the ruling class is, and always has been, the ones that prosper; all others become serfs to the system. As mentioned, open borders are the goal for Re-Setting America into the Final World Empire (Agenda 2030); that way, America gives up her sovereignty.

29

Global Governance Advancing & Famine

Every hour new reports surface on information about the "Establishments" progress on their achievements in setting up their New World System.

As this new information comes forth, I try to keep up; still, keeping up with so much information is hard because everything is advancing speedily; Jesus said all those things would occur at the End of the Age, just as we now witness.

In research, the World Health Organization advocates using vaccine passports under the same internet platform as China's Social Credit System.

China uses facial recognition technology to track and record people's whereabouts, where they work, what they buy online, what websites are visited, and whether they have committed crimes.

The World Health Organization (WHO) utilized Covid 19 to convince the populace to take vaccine passports to travel freely; in the future, they plan to emphasize that to be free, one must be vaccinated and accept a vaccine passport.

Vaccine passports are a simple way for authorities to monitor citizens' movements.

Those who have them will be viewed as outstanding members of society, while those who don't will be stigmatized as undesirable and denied fundamental civil liberties.

Here are several current events that single the establishment of the Final World Empire is near:

- Regarding global governance and population reduction, it is commonly known that some prominent members of the World Economic Forum advocate for global population control.
- Specific individuals concerned about the weather seek to limit the number of cattle that farmers and ranchers can raise, and Bill Gates is developing synthetic meat.
- John Kerry, the Climate Envoy, has pledged to place American agriculture as a "front and center" issue in dealing with the climate agenda, while the Dutch government is planning to dismantle 3,000 farms by "2030 forcibly."
  The UN and WEF are dissatisfied with the rate at which global governance progresses. They aspire to hasten the implementation of their goals, the "2030" agenda, under the Final World Empire.
- Later in the year, the WEF will meet to examine how to speed up the globalist's plans. The report suggests the "Build Back Better Plan" will look a lot like communism.
- Citizens will be expected to put more effort into the "public good" (distribution of wealth among all members of society), not for "individual good."

It would be best to pay more attention to history and the overwhelming effects certain aspects of society had on populations.

One of those significant aspects to be watched is John Kerry and his recent announcement he plans to make agriculture in the United States a "front and center" issue.

Stalin and the Ukrainian Famine

During the worst Ukrainian famine in 1932-1933, people walked the countryside looking for anything to eat; Joseph Stalin ruled the country then.

A young boy in a town in Ukraine saw the nomadic people digging with their bruised hands into areas with vacant gardens looking for something to eat.

Because of such terrible nutritional deficiencies, most people's bodies began to stink and protrude.

Stories are told of people walking about with hollow faces and sunken eyes with no real destination but just out looking for anything to eat, and as they walk, they drop here and there by the wayside.

Overwhelmed doctors placed the bodies on stretchers and tossed them into a massive dug pit.

The Famine Known as the Holodomor

An estimated 3.9 million Ukrainians, or roughly 13% of the population, perished during the Holodomor famine (a word for "starvation and to inflict death").

Natural disasters like pestilence or shortage did not bring on this famine; instead, it resulted from a dictator's desire to replace Ukraine family farms with state-run collectives to penalize Ukrainians who threatened dictatorial control.

A famine brought on by disastrous social-economic policies and directed at a specific group for oppression and control.

Ukraine, a country about the size of Texas situated west of Russia and bordering the Black Sea, was once part of the Soviet

Union. Starlin governed that country and imposed collectivization in 1929 as part of his ambition to rapidly construct a complete communist economy, replacing farms independently operated and owned by a sizeable state-run collective.

Farmers that owned small farms in Ukraine opposed the loss of their land to a communist takeover.

The Soviet government's answer was to label the resisters as "kulaks," or wealthy farmers, who Soviet ideology viewed as state enemies.

Starlin's secret police plotted to deport 50,000 Ukrainian farm families to Siberia, and Soviet officials forcibly evicted the peasants from their land.

Starlin seems to have wanted to change the Ukrainian country into a modern, proletarian, Socialist government, even if it meant killing large parts of the Ukrainian people.

Collectivization didn't go well in Ukraine. By the fall of 1932, the nation's grain harvest missed the target of 60 percent by Soviet planners. As punishment, Starlin ordered the little bit of grain they had to be confiscated for not meeting their quotas.

It caused a massive food crisis and hunger; Stalin's crop collectors used long-wooden poles as they went about the countryside to the peasant's homes to poke the dirt floors and ground around their homes for buried food.

The peasants accused of hiding food were imprisoned, but many were executed in the fields near their homes.

The famine worsened, and many peasants tried to flee in search of other places for more food and died along the wayside.

The peasants were so desperate they had no choice but to eat their pets, bark from trees, roots, grass, leaves, and flowers.

Starlin's adopted policies were proven to be a significant fact; the famine was intentionally created.

As the masses fled their towns and villages to search for food beyond the borders, the communist regime acted with worse measures.

Collective farms, by 1933, only had a third of the families left that did not perish. The labor camps and prisons were overwhelmed.

The Russian government that replaced the Soviet Union claimed the famine did take place but was not genocide.

At least 16 countries prove otherwise, including the United States, in a 2018 report affirming that Stalin committed genocide on his people.

It is best to consider what happened in history when reports come out about officials wanting to tackle a country's food production, as history is shown to repeat itself!

30

Corrupt Narcissistic Rulers

Living under the Final World Empire, Rulers will be influenced by the spirit of the age, the Antichrist spirit, and corruption is everywhere.

Some ways corruption creeps in when Narcissistic rulers are in control:

Society is oppressed under such leaders, which can lead to negative consequences for the people.

A good example is when corrupt politicians seize control of the judicial system and other watchdog agencies to shield themselves from prosecution, and they will take repressive measures to protect their privileges.

Corruption serves the relationship between collective decision-making and the power of the people to affect decisions through voting.

Nefarious societal elements thrive as proceeds can be laundered, funding disguised, and judicial officials and politicians corrupted through bribes (including gifts, favors, and other benefits).

Levels of violence, illegal drugs, prostitution, sex trafficking, kidnapping, and intimidation rise accordingly.

Oppression of the people causes deep suffering; it diminishes lived experiences and divides families, friends, and communities that should be united.

Often oppression overlaps, which causes more intense hardships.

Corruption Affects the Economy

It can significantly affect the targeting of social issues and impact income equality in several ways.

Economies afflicted by an unusually high level of corruption are not capable of prospering as those with a low-level crime.

Corruption, bribes, theft, tax evasion, and other illicit financial flaws cost developing countries 1.26 billion annually.

How Corruption Affects the Poor

It can lead to inefficient allocations of resources, poor education and healthcare, and illegal labor, and can exacerbate social, political, and economic inequality and division; impeding the ability of states to respond to public healthcare or deliver quality education degrades the business environment and undermines the rule of law; in addition, corruption can lead to government institutions and officials not being trusted.

Rule of Law

Corruption damages the economy, affects people experiencing poverty, and can lead to the breakdown of government and diminishes citizens' trust in institutions.

Corrupt systems can coexist with the rule of law, but the rule of law becomes more threatened as corruption increases.

The rule of law is indispensable but not a sufficient coalition for eliminating corruption.

In an uncivilized society, the rule of the jungle or the end justifies the means, even if it is terrible.

Corruption undermines human rights, affecting free speech and not allowing people to protest the wrong done.

Corruption undermines democratic institutions, and weak institutions are less able to control crime.

Western societies have seen an abundance of corruption over the decades, and according to the ancient texts, it will increase worldwide as we move closer to the Final World Empire and Tribulation.

Remember, the Antichrist World leader is called the "Man of Lawlessness" in the scriptures.

31

The Ideology of The Final World Empire

The promoters of The Final World Empire are a group of elite individuals who are believed to be linked to Secret Societies such as the Illuminati, Freemasons, and others.

Such people aim to unite the world under a oneness set of rules and beliefs and to achieve such goals, all nations must adopt the same value system; politically, economically, and socially.

It is essential for a country with a different religious and cultural belief not to adhere to those beliefs but slowly be removed and to have a one-world system of religion that is accepted and honored.

A country with strong spiritual beliefs, such as Christianity and Biblical values, will be slowly phased out because acceptance and tolerance of transgender and homosexuality lifestyles will contradict their Biblical beliefs.

The ideology of The Final World Empire is linked to only one system, it is their ideology, and they will eliminate all opposing viewpoints and beliefs; The One-World system remains the controller and dominant method of value.

Under this world system, economies of all nations will be forced to accept the coming One-World digital currency, which is why all borders are removed by uniting cultures into a global community.

With the current situation of the nation's debt, the coming One-World digital currency will clear all debt as they "Reset" and transform into a digital platform to be embraced by all.

We are seeing careless spending and skyrocketing inflation because they have the "solution" to the problem already entailed; the digital economy will prepare them to be the masterminds that appear to have solved the country and world's problems.

Living under the Final World Empire and trying to maintain a business not operating under the digital platform would end such a business.

Control of an entire world (politically speaking), the countries will be centralized under the Ten-Reginal world areas, with each having a leader over each country allying, and such powerful groups of individuals will be in control of the entire human race in all social, political, and economic decisions.

When those Ten-World rulers appear over the Ten-Reginal areas and are in control, the Antichrist World dictator comes onto the world stage as all Ten-World leaders surrender their power to the Satanic dictator.

Autonomy will cease, and all nations will be centralized into a One-World Economy.

As mentioned, the belief and ideology system behind a One-World Empire is the same value system used to create the Tower of Babel, and the thought process, according to biblical history, is they wanted to unite the world for their common cause.

Those inclined to study ancient texts know and understand

society's outcome of unity without God always results in destruction, as shown in the Tower of Babel's outcome.

Furthermore, a Global society under a One-World system may appear to be an advantage for humanity. Still, the motivational ingenuity that promotes such a belief system should be carefully examined not from just a worldview perspective but a Biblical standpoint would be wise.

As we have explored the Beast system of (Revelation 13), it is the same system currently underway of a group of elites "Resetting" the world system for the Antichrist leader to take center stage.

The Antichrist spirit is the source behind creating such a world system; therefore, the devil prepares the way for the "Lawless One" to come on the scene.

(2 Corinthians 4:4) Refer to Satan as the ruler of this world.

The devil tempted Jesus by showing Him all the world's kingdoms in a moment and told Jesus that if He worshiped him, he would give Jesus all the world's domains and pleasures (Matthew 4:8-10).

Therefore, Satan has tremendous leverage of control over all wrong ideologies, philosophies, religions, and economic systems of the world humanity is currently part of; and he can manage society and influence their cultural and spiritual belief system.

The Final World Empire is at our doorstep, and it is not what the promoters of the One-World global community "resetting" our world system appear to be.

Instead, it will usher in the Great Tribulation with a Satanic Beast system to dominate all earth dwellers, led by the Antichrist.

32

One Health Agenda

Some Proponents of the Final World Empire are collaborating for a crisis to provide a cover for constructing a godless global world government.

They know something big is coming, and it is my opinion; the Rapture of the church will set the world off into panic worldwide; that is something "big" that Must happen, and it is coming!

The World Health Organization (WHO) Assembly meeting discussed these issues in one of their meetings:

They have 300 amendments that the WHO wants to add to the International Health Regulations (IHRs); here are just a few of those things:

- Expand the definitions of pandemic and health emergencies. The WHO can then moderate lockdowns or medical measures solely based on the assumption that a virus might be harmful.
- To ensure that member nations "must follow" and implement

the WHOs proposals, the IHRs recommendations should be binding and no longer nonbinding.

- Stiffen the director general's ability to declare an emergency without other board members agreeing.
- Set up a robust surveillance framework in all member states.
- Make it possible for the WHO to share data from countries without their approval.
- Give the WHO authority over specific resources inside member countries, such as intellectual property rights.
- Coerce countries into following the WHO's lead on censorship.
- Make mandatory all individual-related IHR regulations, such as those concerning the closing of borders, the limitation of travel, quarantines, medical examinations, and the administration of medications and vaccines.

The International Pandemic Treaty that the WHO is pushing:

They want to establish a governing body to manage the entire health emergency procedure under the WHOs authority.

They intend to increase the influence of the WHO by implementing the One Health agenda, which holds the belief that many different aspects of life and the environment might affect one's health and, as a result, can categorize as having the ability to be dangerous. As a result, the World Health Organization will be able to declare the Weather a health emergency (something they have tried to do for years) and, as a direct consequence of it, implement lockdowns, close borders, restrict travel, and so much more.

Modification to the IHR will require a simple majority vote to be accepted for implementation. If the adjustments are adopted, which is widely predicted to happen, member states will have a 10-month window to opt out of receiving the amendments. After that, the new laws and statutes will become effective in May 2025.

The Pandemic Treaty needs the support of two-thirds of the

delegates from the member nations to be ratified. Article 19 of the WHO constitution permits the organization to impose legally binding protocols on all 194 member states if the treaty is accepted.

Following approval from unelected diplomats, the WHOs process" Enables a small number of global representatives to impose international rules on all the WHOs member states, in contrast to how laws are made in most democratic countries, where elected politicians are responsible for enacting national legislation.

The World Health Organization (WHO) is working to tighten its control over global health by rewriting the International Health Organization (IHR) and Pandemic Treaty.

The authority granted to the WHO by the treaty goes well beyond the WHOs present scope of responsibility, which is to respond to epidemics.

The "One Health Agenda" emphasizes human health, animal health, and environmental protection.

Under the "One Health Organization," the WHO is responsible for decisions about diet, agriculture, livestock farming, environmental pollution, population movements, and much more.

Most of the World Health Organization's budget is earmarked or set aside for particular initiatives.

The WHO cannot disperse large sums of money to the needed regions.

In addition to this, it has a considerable impact on the policies and procedures of the WHO.

Therefore, the WHO is an organization that acts following directives provided by the corporations and governments that supply the financing.

The WHO has lost much of its former prominence. To begin, the organization is now largely controlled by powerful business interests.

Bill Gates is the largest single donor to the World Health

Organization thanks to the Gates Foundation and his initiatives like (GAV) the vaccine alliance.

As was previously said, Gates possessed the most wealth and influence and did not sponsor events unless he could profit from them.

For instance, he finances a "green revolution" in Africa that promotes genetically modified (GMO) crops by investing in the companies that produce GMO seeds.

Meanwhile, Gates smiles at the bank while millions go hungry and suffer.

He has a financial interest in immunizations which he supports by participating in efforts to increase vaccination rates.

It has nothing to do with improving the world or assisting other people. He conjures up possibilities for financial investments out of thin air.

The WHO was not the originator of the COVID lockdown approach; instead, this strategy was created independently.

The evidence for this is that the pandemic guidelines in place before the COVID outbreak suggested that afflicted people be quarantined for seven to ten days.

Because of the COVID outbreak, the conventional wisdom was utterly overturned, and people who were healthy and ill were advised to quarantine themselves for several weeks or months.

The WHO is being forced to make that ridiculous and unproven claim.

As a result, much hardship was in place. Family members could not be at the bedside of dying relatives, suicides rose significantly, and young people suffered from depression.

The World Health Organization didn't seem to worry that lockdowns severely hampered several of their worldwide health and well-being goals, especially those related to children.

In addition, the WHO promoted immunization campaigns in

regions with a shallow risk of contracting COVID, such as Africa, despite this knowledge.

Not surprisingly, vaccine-focused organizations funded by Bill Gates, such as (GAV and CEPI) were on the front.

The pandemic industry is putting together the "greatest show on earth." They argue that pandemics are rising; no one knows whether that is true. However, from what we have witnessed thus far, I believe we will see a significant increase in pandemics once the WHO's amendments and other requests are met and put into law in May 2025.

Bill Gates is the WHOs biggest benefactor; it is no surprise that the organization put him in charge of vaccines.

The COVID pandemic fundamentally rewrote the IHR protocols; the United States and the world are also in a precarious position, with the WHOs planning to incorporate and implement their 300 amendments to the IHR.

To summarize, there is a concentrated effort to make the World Health Organization the de facto governing body of the resounding global state under the Final World Empire, which points directly to the Great Tribulation.

While the proponents of the Final World Empire work quickly to establish their modern-day Tower of Babel, their much-planned New World system will come crashing down as God's wrath will utterly destroy their godless society.

It has happened repeatedly throughout Biblical history and is an example for the coming generations.

One thing is sure when a nation casts God out and shakes their fits in His face and renounces His laws and the natural laws of nature, He will allow humanity to have what they 'lust" over, but the ramifications of that choice they made will be damnable beyond any description any mere individual has ever experienced.

Research it for yourself; (Romans 1:21-32).

There have only been two things censored in the country and the world, for that matter: Truth and Obscenity.

Truth has been squashed out here in America, and obscenity is embraced in the culture.

Society calls evil good and good evil now. Some actors and politicians are calling for the banning of Bibles.

Prophecy is being fulfilled, just as predicted, and the "lost" continue to reject God.

Nevertheless, as the ancient text proclaim, we all choose and are responsible for our eternity; I hope you made the right choice.

Jesus is the answer to a lost and dying world.

33

One World Food-Production

As mentioned, the global weather cult uses resources to mitigate a deduction in Arigulculture worldwide.

Thirteen nations are on board with this plan. Countries like the United States, Argentina, Brazil, Chile, and Spain are ample food and livestock producers.

They are among the countries that have agreed to put new limits on farmers to cut methane gas emissions.

As the Global Methane Hub reported, the United States and thirteen other countries signed a commitment to reduce methane emissions.

What matters, and how will it affect the world's citizens?

According to the press release, the Global Methane Hub, along with the Ministries of Agriculture of Spain and Chile, meant together for the first time global conference on agriculture to reduce methane emissions.

High-ranking government officials were invited to attend to share their perspectives. They committed to supporting those efforts in mitigation measures of the farm sector and to collaborate in lowering emissions.

The meeting participants were the UN's Food and Agriculture Organization, the Inter-American Institutes for Corporation of Agriculture, the Climate and Clean Air Coalition, The World Bank, The Inter-American Development Bank, and The Organization for Economic Cooperation and Development.

The UN and the World Bank have lately reported much about a coming world famine.

It is peculiar that at the same time, they are warning about a coming world famine, the UN and World Bank, and the U.S. are preparing to convert to a new and unproven form of farming that reduces emissions.

Australia, Brazil, Burkina Faso, Czech Republic, Ecuador, Germany, and Panama are other countries that signed onto the transformation of farming policies.

Their Agenda, they must save the planet from cow farts as it is the cause of emissions, so they must change to farmland converting their livestock and land to more innovative methods.

They have been claiming the old way of farming will be changed to “new technologies” and science-based. However, they never tell us what those science-based new technologies are.

For years, the UN, World Economic Forum, and other NGOs have promoted replacing meats, chicken, dairy cows, and pork with mealworms, insect larvae, crickets, etc.

Massive insect factories that billionaires have invested in are being built in the state of Illinois, Canada, and the Netherlands, where mealworms, crickets, and other bugs will be processed as additives to be implemented into the food supply, often not labeled to inform the public of what their eating.

Bio-Tech Foods, the largest meat manufacturer in the world, is planning to construct a factory in Spain to create one thousand metric tons of artificial beef annually, according to a report on June 13, 2023.

The billionaires, who are leading contributors, are investing in lab-grown meat, which is a process that involves cancer cells from cows, pigs, and chickens to grow synthetic beef at a fast pace.

Natural farming has existed since time, and God still controls His planet and creation.

Narcissism is Rising! The modern-day Tower of Babel builders are not gods, even though they have openly proclaimed that they are above most of humanity, as John Kerry referenced at the World Economic Summit.

The Weather is a "cover" being utilized by billionaires to reconstruct, transform, and dismantle the natural laws of God and nature.

With everything, there is a cycle. Those that want to know and learn the "truth" about the fate of this country and the world will find answers to those concerns in the ancient texts; the Bible is clear on this.

The world will continue to exist if there is a beginning and an end. Seed and harvest, cold and heat, summer and spring shall not cease by night or day. As long as the planet remains, there will be sowing and reaping, cooling and heating, spring and fall, summer and winter, morning and evening. These things will continue on all the days of the earth and never change (Genesis 8:22); explain this.

An engineered global famine is in the making and conducted by wealthy individuals, mostly atheists, who no longer want us to live naturally and freely and look to God as our "source."

They have meant and started another "new initiative," a "One-World Agriculture" production, that they believe we no longer need to eat the meats and foods created by the Almighty, but that they have a "better way" than He in doing things!

I don't know how you feel about this matter. Still, my opinion is that brazing, smug, narcissistic atheists have decided they intend us to eat their factory-grown bugs and synthetic meats that they claim are better for the planet.

God is the "ONLY ONE" who decides the outcome of the earth, and not a group of wealthy individuals who have an "opposing nature" toward the Highest.

It is all part of the insanity of Narcissism, as I just recently finished writing another book on the subject.

When you factor in all those many things the billionaires are doing to transform our world into their godless, global society, there is nothing there that is favorable toward the culture that shows any signs of "aiding' people to live a more productive, and healthy lifestyle; it will bring only misery, bondage, starvation, and death.

It would be best to accept the "truthful facts" and not ignore the circumstances that godless individuals lie and tell us what is best for humanity.

God holds the earth in His hands, and unregenerated, depraved narcissists will not "save" the planet. To believe what they tell you is accurate; is to think that God cannot manage His creation.

Only three things can bring depopulation; War, famine, and Plagues are the most efficient ways to do so.

Don't you find it interesting that all three methods are being orchestrated now?

The assault on health and food is similar to what is occurring in the energy sector, where governments are consorting with giant corporations to convert our methods of mobility to ones that are powered by electric energy, even though the vast majority of the general population will not be able to purchase electric vehicles.

Those who can afford electric cars will be subject to strict regulations because charging stations drain an already stressed power grid.

If you need to charge your car and can only do so at specified times, your mobility is effectively controlled by the power grid administrators.

In the Netherlands, the war on food is already in full swing. They plan to cut the number of farm animals by half and the number of nitrogen fertilizers by thirty percent.

All the talk about new tools and innovation is just that: talk. They say that farms will increase their revenue. The question is, what farms and who owns them? If they are government-owned farms, I believe that is an accurate statement.

All their new and creative technologies result in famine; and, as a result, starvation.

You are hearing terms like; You will own nothing and be happy; you will live where they assign you and share your cubical space with another family when you are not home; They have new technologies and innovations in farming to save the planet; You don't need your car you are driving anymore because of greenhouse gases, so buy an electric powered one, or take the transit, ride your bike or walk. You will have a protein-rich diet of insects; keep your thermostat in your cubical shared apartment at 78 degrees; it does not matter if you live where the summers average 90-100s. Yes, you heard right; because reports have circulated, it is coming. As a parent, you have no right to object to what your children are taught in public schools; once they enter the school grounds, they are the state's property. Michigan and Minnesota have alerted parents already on this matter.

At this current time frame in the country, we are already seeing what civilization will be like by 2030.

Globalists are increasing their planned global governance agenda to completion, perhaps before 2030.

It is the Final World Empire, led by a deceiver; whoever their chosen man is, he will be the Beast of Revelation 13, the Antichrist.

34

A Depraved Narcissistic Mindset

Living under the Final World Empire will be anything but ordinary, which is why we are seeing such a Rise in Narcissism, which is getting worse as each day passes.

Some political class members hold a copy of the book, "Rules for Radicals," which they admire despite its devilish tone, and the author is a criminal.

I became aware a few decades ago of their extremist methods as I began researching this new utopia they plan to create.

Never before did I believe I would see such an onslaught of wickedness as we currently witness in our culture.

Just as God threatened to do in (Romans1), it appears He has done so to many people of prominence by turning them over to a reprobate mindset, allowing them to engage in evil behaviors, such as deception, fraud, and sexual perversion, an anomaly that is only just getting started compared to what the results will be under the godless one-world system they are creating.

It is impossible to reason with such people by pointing them in the right direction and telling them they are wrong.

Because these people are malignant narcissists, they will not listen to your talk.

They operate under incorrect emotions the entire time because that is what narcissists do.

It is best not to converse with these people but to ignore them and walk away.

Selfish people like these and other extremists prioritize protecting the environment over human life.

When you hear a speech that claims to be honest and benevolent toward its citizens but values lifeless objects more than human life, there is something seriously wrong with that perspective.

Malignant Narcissistic people constantly lie and take from others, and Jesus tells us, "To not cast our pearls before swine."

The Lord is referring to (pearls of truth and knowledge). They will never accept your guidance and truthful facts.

The state of our country is in severe deterioration.

After the mental facilities, we're emptied of the mentally ill; some rose to power and have used secret agents for surveillance on those who have not committed any crimes.

We are currently witnessing (Romans 1:22-32) being enacted.

Furthermore,

The Bible warns against the consequences of sexually grooming very young children, but some see nothing wrong and believe it's ok to do such things.

Children are the greatest gift from God, yet many treat children with contempt or even objects to exploit sexually.

Those who do such things and give permission to do this are

under the wrong mindset of which (Romans 1:22-32) speak about being given over to a reprobate mindset.

They will stand before God and give an account for their disturbing and wicked perversions by destroying young children.

It is written that it would be better if they were never born since they harm a child. Jesus said, "A millstone should be tied around the neck of such people and tossed into the deepest ocean."

Such people have no fear of the Almighty, and God has laid out for us what is sinful, and He tells us no one is without excuse. He says, "The heavens declare the glory of God," proving His eternal power.

Some churches have allowed what God calls sinfulness to go unnoticed. They are more concerned with the "numbers in the church than preaching what God calls sin.

The creatures of darkness tell ordinary people to their faces, "We're coming after your children."

God's all-consuming fire of His wrath will consume such people.

It is critical, especially in this current era when "insanity" is running wild in the hearts and minds of some people, that you vigorously guard your children and never let them out of your sight.

The creatures of darkness do not respect God's most precious, the children.

We are witnessing Narcissism Rising more dangerously than ever before in this country now that children are being exploited and sexualized in many ways.

It is up to all of us to stand for the most innocent, the children, because there is nothing left but the children for the demonic realm to capture.

Don't hand your children over to the dark creatures of the night and agree with the mentally ill that are slithering around to harm the children by telling them it is ok to do the unthinkable. Those that are predators of children have already lost any sanity they may have once had. They have now been given over to a reprobate mindset.

35

America's Freedom's Fall

Today a country that was once founded on Biblical principles as the founding fathers set a precedent for us; is now the murder, pornography, and perversion capital.

The enemy is inside the gate, and the root of evil is firmly entrenched in the land.

Palm 127 tells of the demise of a nation when they reject God, and we are witnessing the realities of the destruction of a country and its deterioration.

It is no longer "God Bless America" that is in progress, and our current everyday situation as a nation is in contrast to America's history (in obedience to God), which is now in open rebellion and rejection of any of the values it was founded upon.

During (the 1960s) the decline of the country became increasingly prominent, and the Bible was no longer used as a foundation of learning and prayer as it once was.

As mentioned, the schools and universities removed the Bible, and a long-time social decline began and has never recovered; considering the wickedness that society seems to embrace currently, the nation has fallen.

Looking back throughout the pages in time, within just a few decades, it is recognizable and prominent, the progressive measures of decline in the moral structure of the nation.

God has pronounced judgment on any country that harms children in any way.

When the ancient text tells us that "Children are the heritage from God, and His reward is the fruit of the womb, it is telling us the "value" that the Highest puts on His children, and Jesus many times indicated that abuse of His children would bring harsh ramifications.

What are children being taught? And what will a country endure when it proclaims "under the rights of a child" that minors be subjected to gender surgeries and puberty blockers, and parents have no rights or say so?

I hope you understand my point. It is not about equal rights for children; it is about depopulation.

Children that have the surgeries will not be able to reverse it and will not be able to reproduce.

Parents need to understand this, and everything being torn down and transformed in the country is for one reason; it is an agenda that narcissistic reprobates are using to advance their Final World Empire.

America's enemies have arrived, and they are increasing daily.

The country is fighting for its very existence, and many of our freedoms are censored or lost; a once mighty nation is slowly being dismantled, and the children are the targets of lunatics in high places.

The Christians will also be their target once the Narcissistic world leader is in control, maybe sooner, as things are already going in that direction.

The demon of tyranny is working overtime to suppress all freedoms we once had, and those in hi gh places understand America still has a "spark" of freedom left, yet, they are working feverishly to squish it out.

Freedom has always been a cornerstone of the human spirit throughout the world, but because of greed, money, and power, it is severely compromised.

Please understand completely; This nation is the focus of wealthy narcissistic individuals that hate America and are doing everything they can to destroy it.

Without America as a free country, all other countries outside the nation will rapidly submit to a one-world system.

The crushing of our freedoms and all resistance is to a totalitarian regime that will ultimately establish their new world system, the Final World Empire.

36

Revived Sodom

A century ago, there was a fear of God in people's hearts and minds, and as Romans 3:8 says, There is no fear of God in their minds, meaning They are bold like the men of Sodom; they openly yelled out filth to Lot to open the door so they could sexually assault the two angels God sent to get Lot out of Sodom before He destroyed it, with fire and brimstone falling from the sky.

Today those same fundamentals of Sodom dare the God of the universe to oppose them.

Narcissism is Rising! And reflecting the "core nature" of those who do such things.

America has now become a revived Sodom and has plunged into wickedness like never before.

We have crossed the finish line of God tolerating transgressions for His mercy's sake.

We live in dark times, and the days are getting more wicked, just as foretold; just before the Lord returns, the world will plunge into incredible darkness and be as in the days of Lot and Noah.

It will become so severe that it will become unstoppable until the Lord defeats it when He returns.

Promoters of the Rainbow Jihad

As I researched how the Rainbow Jihad movement has advanced, I thought you might want to know who financially supports this movement.

The three most essential and primary factors are Black Rock, Vanguard, and State Street, the three most prominent investment firms.

These corporations influence assets worth $20 trillion, and they can coerce businesses into adopting sexual diversity policies because they sit on multiple boards and hold millions of shares in various companies.

In the meantime, federal agencies have been falling over themselves to support queer activism but don't acknowledge the sacrifice of those who served in the military to ensure their freedoms.

When the truth is seized, the entire world is thrown into chaos. Yet, it is the fulfillment of the Bible telling us that society will deteriorate just before and during the Final World Empire. This present culture is being transformed into a community run by delusional thinkers that collude on the best way to dismantle a nation so that Narcissism will be the dominating force in those ruling the earth, just before and during the rule of the coming world dictator, the Beast.

Everyone has the right to choose how they want to live and the lifestyle that goes along with it; that is between them and God.

The problem is, however, when specific individuals refuse to have that same belief for others. They don't hesitate to try and enforce their ideologies and opinions on other people but try and shut them down if they don't conform to their ways.

As mentioned previously, there are only two "views" people can choose from.

A "world view" and a "Biblical world view."

It has always been that way since the beginning of time, and it will never change, despite how much specific individuals despise that some people in the world hold to a "Biblical worldview."

The sooner they can grasp this, the quicker they will come to terms with the fact that others have different values and standards they live by.

Committed Christians are a small minority in this current culture who hold a "Biblical worldview," no one will ever cause them to deny their faith and Jesus as their Savior.

These people are willing to lay down their life if that be the case, and let me explain why. Jesus said if anyone denies Him, He will deny that person, and such a person does not stand a chance of entering Heaven if that be the case; once again, it all comes down to a personal choice, and if specific individuals choose to hold to a "Biblical world view" no one will ever cause them to reject that. It is just that simple, and particular individuals should accept that others also have their rights and opinions. It's time for some to stop being playground bullies and grow up.

It would be best in the long run and eternal future of some, to leave the Christians alone because nothing will ever squish them out, and yes, it is a reality; some may have to die for their belief in this current culture, the bible is quite clear on this, yet, they will gladly choose that, over rejecting their Lord, Jesus Christ because that will never happen.

Even though many will try to cancel out Christians to silence, it will never take place, and living under the Final World Empire, the hatred for believers will be severe, yet, God is always with us, despite the hate of those who willingly choose to reject the Son of God and not live by the values He set in place for those who love Him above everything else.

Sooner or later, such people must accept the "Truth."

"Am I your enemy because I tell you the truth" (Galatians 4:16)?

37

Concerning Aspects of the Final World Empire

There are now 34 people serving on the Executive Board of the World Health Organization.

It is now out in the open that a representative from North Korea will be serving on the Executive Committee of the WHO for the following three years.

North Korea is a communist dictatorship that allegedly starves its population, runs prison camps, kills citizens for political opposition, arbitrarily detains citizens without legal representation, and more.

In addition, North Korea reportedly possesses nuclear weapons.

It baffles the mind that leaders of the world would intrust authority on a global scale to someone from a communist country, North Korea.

The World Health Organization has announced intentions to establish a worldwide system known as the "Global Digital Health

Certification Network (GDHCN) to monitor population mobility, vaccination coverage, and other data points of interest.

The EU has established a framework (the Digital Covid Certificate) to facilitate this in European Member states.

The European Union and the World Health Organization convened a press conference and announced their intention to collaborate on a plan to make the European Union healthcare system genuinely global.

It is a precursor for control during the Final World Empire.

The reason is it would make it possible to monitor and restrict the movement of individuals throughout the world. Because it also can do what we saw happen during the Covid trial, which is to prevent people from purchasing and selling unless they can provide digital proof that they have had a specific type of medical treatment; it would do both, and this has never happened before in the archives of human history anywhere in the planet. It was unheard of, yet few Christian leaders acknowledged it for what it was.

The nazis used a similar system in their health network to track people and those considered undesirable and others with mental disabilities, etc.

People had to carry their papers everywhere they went during Hitler's reign. If you didn't have your documents on you when you were stopped for whatever reason, the nazis put such people in prison, or other extreme measures were used.

It is the same tracking system the EU and World Health Organization are implementing.

The one-world beast system of the Final World Empire is creeping in under the pretext of our "health," with frequent "health checks" required to operate in society.

Those who refuse to comply will be sought out and labeled as enemies of the system and, hence, a threat to humanity.

We have already witnessed on news channels that those who did not receive specific medical treatment during Covid were considered a threat to others.

It was their trial run.

The real deal is coming! It is merely the beginning foundation of a structure that, in the long run, will alter how everyone on earth lives and carries out their daily activities.

Just as the nazis implemented their system, and this wicked structure emanated from Europe, it is the same: the restored Roman Empire, described in the Book of Daniel, and the Final World Empire.

Concerning Deception

The World Economic Forum (WEF) official Yuval Noah Harari believes there might be a correct religion in a few years because they will use holy books that Artificial Intelligence writes."

Remember, this is an open attack against two of the major religions in the world: Christianity, Judaism, and the Bible.

Yuval Noah Harari is Jewish and openly opposes God and the Bible in many of his messages on his youtube channel and other websites.

Jesus warned about such people concerning the culture of the Final World Empire and said, first and foremost, Deception in the world will be rampant just before He Returns. He told us not to be deceived because false prophets will be spreading false messages and even doing what looks like a miracle that will fool some believers because of their ignorance and not knowing what is in the letter of Truth He and the prophets spoke about.

Furthermore, read Revelation 13:15, And he (the false prophet) had the power to give the image of the beast (a talking robot image of the Antichrist) life and that it should be able to talk, causing all that refuse to bow down to the talking image should be executed.

Suppose a talking robot statue (Al) is programmed to produce (what they want to call holy scriptures) for their new One World Global Religion. Isn't it probable that the Antichrist's authorities will call for the execution of any earth dweller through (Al) that does not bow down and worship the talking image, Al?

The Bible proclaims that this talking image of the Beast, Antichrist, will cause anyone who does not surrender in worship to the image to be executed.

In addition, many will go to their eternal doom because they refused the "factual truths" of the genuine "Words of Truth" in the Bible.

Do not be deceived by this new talking image of the Antichrist erected in the Jerusalem Temple during the Tribulation, when the Antichrist regime will be the new government of the world under the Final World Empire.

Jesus prophesies that all these things will be fulfilled. It is best to pay attention to the warnings before it is too late.

38

A Rogue Regime

A rogue regime is considered an "outlaw state," and the Final World Empire fits that description.

Why? Governments that are dictatorships or totalitarian and violate the human rights of their citizens are rogue regimes.

The leaders of such a regime freely commit crimes and always "deflect" blame on someone else being responsible for the very crimes they commit.

Leaders of such a regime will masquerade around as if to show they have the best interest of its citizens.

If a once-free country is overcome by a rogue regime, it will surrender its national sovereignty. It will dismantle programs and policies set in place by its predecessors.

A deceptive rescue plan is instituted with promises of showing a Better Way, only to deceive its citizens.

Violent crimes, gangs, drug trafficking, and death are all part of a rogue regime; nothing will stop it if it is used to serve a specific purpose of such a regime.

If anything conflicts with a narrative, ideology, plan, or agenda, even if it is "true," it will be removed from the public sector.

News outlets, social media networks, and radio are usually controlled by a rogue regime, and this way, no one is responsible for the crimes they commit under its leadership because there is no accountability; thus, propaganda is presented to the public and not truthful reporting, but misinformation.

Lies are presented to the public under a rogue regime; the dictators expect the misinformation the people hear to be accepted, no questions asked; if so, they will be dealt with accordingly, and this is how they gain control over their citizens and by doing so, they control all news outlets.

A rogue regime that functions in such a way is under the leadership of an intolerant Neo-Marxist.

Unbearable debt, an increasing number of homeless, and sick and addicted people living on the streets; meanwhile, Marxist leaders and their families live in luxury, have the best education for their children, and starvation is not a problem with such people.

The ordinary people living under a rogue regime will suffer unemployment, a deteriorating healthcare system, and a paralyzed citizenry because of such hardships.

A Rogue Justice System.

A rogue justice system is always used under a rogue nation, and they will put people in their justice system loyalists to their Marxist party.

They do not allow dissent, and anyone who challenges their law will be held accountable and tried by a lawless selected judge and jury and convicted and sentenced to prison; some are even assassinated in jail, such as in high-profile cases that threaten them.

Such people are skilled in deception and "mask" their corruption under the pretense of their citizens.

These individuals are malignant narcissists because they commit crimes without remorse, and everything they say is a lie.

They have no regard for human life, so they can use genocide on their people to eradicate them for whatever suits them at the time.

Such people are free to commit high crimes if anything stands in the way of their planned agenda, knowing they never have to account for their corruption.

Marxist leaders under a rogue regime always have a smile on their faces in front of the camera and are so brave with hypocrisy that their Narcissistic mannerism radiates for all the world to see.

When a once-free country is overtaken by a rogue regime, most will not be aware of the damage done until it is too late and all freedoms have been removed.

Many of those citizens watched their country being transformed in phases, and as each stage in that transformation was complete, another change took place, yet, they remained silent.

Just as Jewish people in Poland during World War11 were taken over by the nazis and transferred to the "Polish gulag," they watched daily a brick wall being built around them until one day the wall was complete, and they were boxed in, not able to come or go freely.

Those living in the "Polish gulag" froze to death, and many died of starvation and illness, not having a doctor to treat them. People lay dead in the streets, and young children cried for food, stomachs protruding.

The suffering and death under the Narcissistic, demonic Hitler regime were in the millions, yet, most of the world remained silent, even though they knew about the crematories.

As long as citizens remain silent and witness a rogue regime occupying their country with little to no resistance, they, too, will experience the same conditions that those in the "Polish Gulag" endured.

Jesus warned us that such conditions would be like living under the

Final World Empire. He also told us that hazardous situations would increase as we rapidly approach the "Blessed Hope," the Rapture.

As mentioned, business as usual will be conducted by the average person right up until that day; once it occurs, everything is kicked into high gear concerning the plans of those who are proponents of the Final World Empire, and the satanic world dictator comes out into the spotlight on the world stage.

This Final World Empire will make all other "rogue regimes" look minor in comparison. It will be the ultimate Rogue Regime with daily evil intentions toward those fortunate enough to survive.

39

They are Speeding Up Their Global Efforts

There is a push to speed up the implementation of global government.

The May 2023 summit of the World Health Organization discussed much at their meeting.

They unleashed an incredible bombshell just one week after the WHO meeting ended.

The European Union has allegedly devised a global digital passport regulating our health conditions and access to transportation.

In essence, this global digital passport would be a QR code generated by your mobile phone, and scanning it would indicate whether or not the bearer is following the requirements set forth by the World Health Organization, granting them the right to travel and freedom of movement.

It is the first step toward combining your digital health records once it assumes control of the European digital passport.

In the future, your entire existence will be encoded in a single QR code.

In June 2023, the digital passport is now valid around the world.

Worse yet, the corporate media has overlooked chiefly this critical developing story.

The consequences of this passport for the country and world are far-reaching.

Our routines will be radically altered within the next 12 months.

We're looking less than one year from now for the total worldwide digital passport to be enforced on everyone worldwide.

We are well past when the passport was conceived; it exists now!

All that needs to be done is to gather support from all nations on this initiative.

Nobody from corporate media is discussing this enormous restriction that will come into effect regarding our privacy and our rights to travel.

This information is only circulating at this time through non-mainstream media.

The duties of a watchman or watchwomen are out of Ezekiel 33.

It is up to those who heed the warning message that the watchmen & women declare.

The duty of those warnings is to sound the alarm; they are not responsible for ensuring that the people will listen.

The corporate media tends to underreport developing dangers around the globe, despite these dangers being real and on the move.

For those of the "true followers" of Jesus living in these dark times, it's important to "watch" the signs of the times as our Lord commanded us to and stay grounded in the bible to understand what is taking place.

God is in control, and we are not to be fearful if we are part of the body of Christ.

If you do not know Jesus personally as your Lord and Savior, now would be an excellent time to ask Him to forgive your sins and become Lod and Savior of your life.

According to prophecy, we understand the world will get darker as time passes.

Jesus is the world's light, and all that follow Him walk in His light and have nothing to fear but warn as many as we can before it is too late.

The clock is ticking and approaching only seconds before mid-night when Christ returns to gather His remnant of believers in the glorious event, the "Blessed Hope," just as He promised in the holy scriptures at the Rapture of His people.

Once this occurs, the Tribulation begins during the Final World Empire.

Be Ready!

40

A Spiritual Battle

Tyrannical and Powerful unbelievers are imposing their false religious beliefs on this country, and a world without God is their foundation in transforming the planet.

We are in a battle, and it is a war between spiritual light and spiritual darkness.

Sadly, many people are not paying attention to what appears to be a battle for the soul of this nation.

A massive populace is AWOL in this battle for the country, and most are just going about without thinking about the future because they are drinking, eating, marrying, and doing everything they did in Noah's day; as the ancient text tells us, they will do until it is too late for them.

There still is a remnant of people who the texts tell us are pilgrims just passing through this world, looking for a city ruled by truth and righteousness; King Jesus is their Savior.

These people have the discernment to recognize where the spiritual battle we are in the midst of originates from.

Satan and his emissaries focus on God's remnant people in spiritual warfare. If the enemy can get us to let our guard down, all will be overtaken by this blanket of evil spreading like wildfire worldwide.

All God's warriors must be full of His spirit and clothed in God's armor because the gremlins are out to destroy and impose their wickedness on as many truth-tellers as possible.

It is essential for God's remnant people to always be on the lookout and alert with perseverance, praying, and the shield of faith to defect all the attack arrows sent to destroy by God's enemy, Satan.

We still have a small window of opportunity open to proclaim the warning that danger is coming by the henchmen from the abyss, to captivate all souls of humanity, and boldly proclaim that Jesus has prepared a way of escape from eternal doom once the Tribulation begins, living under the Final World Empire.

We are Ambassadors for Jesus, and the spiritual battle here in this country and world is intensifying as the hounds from hell have launched an offensive to captivate all humanity and take as many to hell with them as possible.

The gremlins are marching in the street, boldly telling us; they are coming for our children, and if that is not enough to motivate a wake-up call, then all is lost!

It is hard to imagine that wickedness will be worse than we witness today.

Tyrannical and Powerful unbelievers are launching an all-out attack on today's culture.

They gleefully smile, telling us boldly what their intentions are and will not stop until they have completed their warfare upon humanity and the destruction of civilization.

Such powerful unbelievers are using every means possible to destroy the traditional world we grew up in and are familiar with, rebuild according to their lusts for greed and power, and enslave all earth dwellers under their Final World Empire.

It is why we see unrelenting lawlessness, extreme perversion of depraved individuals, haters of God and His order to live by, and a Narcissistic mindset.

Such forces of evil can entrap the vulnerable because they are unaware of the traps set for them.

Still, God's "truth" is freely moving in His people as they proclaim liberty to the captive, as His truth marches on.

The Final World Empire will be the end of this world we all are familiar with, and any plan of escape will no longer be possible without severe suffering and possible death for those seeking refuge during that era.

41

Everything Falling into Place

There is a call to action to transform the way we live proposed by the UN and is geared toward establishing a communist-style centralized government with absolute power.

Under the 2030 Agenda, the Final World Empire, claims are made it will abolish poverty, famine, poor health, lack of education, and environmental degradation.

In brief, the UN wants to impose new laws, regulations, projects, and initiatives for everyone to achieve 17 "Sustainability" goals they believe are best for the earth.

It all sounds like a great thing on the surface.

We must care for the earth, and the impoverished and outcasts are the ones we must assist.

War, violence, and human suffering must end, and all diseases must be treated and eventually abolished.

Of course, all reasonable people would agree to these policies, and everyone should want to see these things accomplished, don't you agree?

Wrong. It illustrates the point precisely. The Philosophy of "Sustainability" or "Environmentalism" should have the backing of individuals of all backgrounds, beliefs, and political persuasions.

In other words, if they can persuade all the people on earth to work together toward the goal of "Sustainability," they can achieve their ultimate goal: the unity of the world.

Those who know the scriptures should understand that God's warning for these Last Days is for humanity to unite politically, economically, and spiritually (Revelation 13) under a global government, economy, and a one-worldwide faith.

I agree that we should take care of the world God gave us, and the ancient texts make it quite clear that we are responsible for the things God entreats to us.

Similarly, I agree with helping the needy, sick, and oppressed; however, uniting humanity under a global government that is anti-God of the Bible is vastly different regarding serving God under the authority of a worldwide government.

The point, when the Antichrist finally does make his appearance, he will not be trying to establish a global government right away; when he is crowned world leader, he immediately will have command over a unified planet since the Final World Empire will be ready and waiting for him.

Starting the process of building an empire at the beginning of the seven-year Tribulation would be too time-consuming; therefore, the world leader cannot appear until all the prerequisites have been met.

All the pieces must be in place during a chess game, and this is precisely what Agenda 2030 is all about.

This new set of global goals is a significate step forward for the UN, which has been steadily gaining influence since it implemented Agenda 21 (essentially a first draft of Agenda 2030) in 1992 at a summit in Rio de Janeiro.

As mentioned, the objective of the UN looks excellent on paper;

the difficulty, however, is that its true purpose is to give the United Nations even more remarkable power over people's lives.

Some of their objectives:

How to eradicate poverty? Spread the wealth around.

The Ecosystem protection? Gradually re-introduce urban dwellers to the city in small, more energy-efficient, eco-friendly residential complexes.

Cut back on electricity? Install smart meters in people's living cubicles and regulate their power usage.

Make Education more accessible. Spread the Common Core curriculum worldwide to the lower class while the powerful and oppressive unbelievers have the best education for their children.

Reduce food insecurity? Replace GMOs and lab-grown meats only for the lower class, not the powerful and authoritative unbelievers.

Such objectives will pave the way for legislation that will give the Final World Empire, a global government, influence over every facet of our life.

It is an excellent strategy for establishing a global government, and Satan is the mastermind over the entire Agenda.

Whether people want to acknowledge it or not, our globe is swiftly nearing the time that Jesus and the prophets predicted when it would be united.

This event is halfway through completion, but most humanity does not want to recognize the fact.

As the UN implements Agenda 2030, freedoms will quickly be eradicated, and the U.S. Constitution will be replaced with a Global Constitution.

After this takes place, it will only take a specific event; possible war, famine, economic collapse, terrorism, another plague, but the most significant event, I believe will be the vanishing of millions of people at the Rapture, to cause complete chaos and terror in the hearts of humanity to cry out for a leader to take control and bring peace; the Antichrist regime of Revelation 13.

The coming world leader, the Antichrist, is personified in chapter 13 of Revelation as a beast that rises out of the sea and has the name of blasphemy on its head.

Satan will elevate the antichrist to a position of great authority, and people will worship Satan and the beast, those living on earth at the time whose names are not written in the Book of Life. Read (Revelation 13:8).

Countless people will submit and agree to have their lives controlled by the global leader by the principles of the 2030 Agenda under the Final World Empire.

It will be a hopeless endeavor, though, only lasting three-and-one-half years because every human initiative is ultimately perverted because of Satan's influence.

The modern nations of our time will unite, forming that Final Empire, and the UN is speedily becoming a formation of such a government with the soon-to-be dividing into ten regional world areas.

They have already established the world court, world bank, world economics, coming world currency, world military, which is the world peacekeeping force, and soon coming one-world religion.

The antichrist will rise to power under the advocacy of peace. Once the Rapture takes place, the world will be plunged into total unsolved panic, and people will be horrified that millions have vanished; this is when the Beast unites the world under peace, but it will be a false peace!

To subjugate every nation and conquer the world, the antichrist, and false prophet will have a massive army that will cause immense damage to the planet. (Revelation 13, Daniel 7:7, 23).

Both tyrants will be influential in establishing their world religion, powered by Satan, using Al as their Holy Book.

42

The Downward Spiral Acceleration

There are striking parallels between the current state of the world, the Book of Daniel, and other prophetic writings in the Old Testament.

World situations must culminate for the prophecies of the Seventy Weeks of Years to be fulfilled (Daniel 9:22-27), which are significant.

The prophet Daniel is shown by the Lord the 70 weeks, broken into three sections: Seven weeks of years, sixty-two weeks of years, and one last week of seven years.

The first two phases have been completed, combining 69 weeks.

The time of the Tribulation, also known as the Time of Jacobs Trouble, is found in Revelation 4:1 and lasts for the final week of seven years.

We are not told how long it takes from the end of the 69 weeks until the beginning of the last week (seven-year tribulation). Still, it's reasonable to believe it spans from the time of Jesus's crucifixion and the establishment of the church age until the appearance of the world dictator, the Beast.

We live in the Church Age; roughly two thousand years have passed, and to fully understand how fast the prophecies are fulfilled, research the New Testament.

Matthew 24, Mark 13, and Luke 21 clearly explain events that "must" occur before the end of this age, during the Final World Empire, and we are witnessing such events daily on news outlets and social media.

One of the essential prophecies is humanity's degenerative conditions on a personal level, which the Apostle Paul warned about in (2 Timothy3:1-7).

It is impossible to overlook the quickening pace of such a catastrophic turn which has been progressively accelerating since the 1960s.

As a result of that era, aggressive and deviant behavior has increased dramatically.

There is a vast difference between the 60s and the current culture, and the difference in cultural thinking and understanding in the entertainment industry makes it evident that the spiral downfall of society and culture is an unfortunate reality.

It is now possible for humans to deceive, dominate, and oppose other humans on a vast scale, thanks to technological advancement and using it for unethical and evil purposes. There has been a rapid decline in the past couple of years.

Everything points to events currently being fulfilled, as we are warned in Revelation 13 about the "mark" everyone "Will" take to be able to buy and sell.

Once millions of believers vanish in the Pre-Tribulation Rapture, the complete rule over humanity will kick into high gear.

The soon-coming demise of our current cash system and the new digital currency to replace it, already being formulated, is the likely channel to be used to control all humanity.

America was given a reprieve in 2016 for a short time, and the pushback from that delayed the powerful and degenerate oligarchs in their completion of world governance.

In 2023, the oligarchs announced an emergency meeting to discuss accelerating their completion of the 2030 Agenda, the Final World Empire.

Their new empire is moving at incredible speed, and nothing will delay their advancement in their dream of building their empire again.

The corporate-led group of influential world influence builders is noticing that people are starting to feel the effects of the domination and dismantling of their freedoms, organized food shortages, and loss of heating of their homes on a grand scale.

The oligarchs understand that people are beginning to feel desperate, and drastic measures will be applied as it continues to worsen and rebellion of the people takes place.

The increased measures that the Tower of Babel builders take to speed up their actions indicate that the Final World Empire will soon be complete, and the one most crucial event holding them back in preparing the way for their leader to come on center stage is the Rapture has not yet happened. Still, once it does, everything falls into place at an incredible speed.

43

Did You Ever Expect It to Happen In Your Lifetime

Did you ever expect to see changes in the culture when you were a young adult as you see them now?

The Western world honors every abnormal behavior possible. We are now presented with claims of men being able to breastfeed and have babies.

As mentioned, little children are being taught it is ok to3 be mutilated and change their gender.

America should be on her knees, repenting and begging God for His forgiveness of the deviant lifestyle trending in the streets of this country.

Did you ever expect that most politicians would work for their cause that benefits their plans and that we, the people, would foot the bill?

Did you ever expect in your life that most of our representatives would favor a world government at the expense of the people losing their freedoms and liberty?

I did not expect in my lifetime that AI would be teaching at specific Ivy League universities and surpassing the intelligence of humans.

Strong similarities could be linked to the days of Noah and our day; the only difference is we have technology.

Anyone who has been watching the "signs of the times" knows that America could not remain the world's superpower and has been in the process of decline for world government to be established; however, did you ever expect to see her fall at such a rapid rate?

Did you ever expect to see a leader of a free country as a negative attraction to the world, and the country's safety is in question?

God says in the scriptures that, He sets up men in high places and removes them. So, it is fair to say such people are put in place to fulfill the prophecy for God to usher in His wrath on an unbelieving world.

Did you ever expect that influential and tyrannical people would induce starvation and shut down farms in the name of climate?

Whoever expected to see in their life that lockdowns are a part of everyday life? It started with Covid lockdowns, and many have reported that climate lockdowns are coming.

Which is the right mantra, "You will own nothing and be happy," or is it, "You will travel nowhere and be happy"? I guess it can be both, this late anyway!

I did not expect that people of faith would be considered outdated and a despicable feature, holding others back from progressing in their cause. Nonetheless, that is an ongoing prophecy concerning the times before the Rapture of God's faithful remnant.

It is faith in God that was the bedrock of this nation. God once blessed. It is no longer the case, as now we are reaping the effects of sin on a God-rejecting world.

The prophecy tells us that the days you and I are living in will be dangerous and filled with corruption and violence; from the top and spreading throughout society.

As mentioned, we are living in Romans 1 day. Society is given over to a depraved mindset, just as the prophets predicted.

(11Timothy3) Tells us they will ignore the truth and choose evil; they will embrace unnatural things because they no longer have natural affection. Their mind has been turned over to doing such things because, knowing the truth, they chose to walk away and embrace the unnatural.

Those that do this are in a dangerous situation; they have already lost their soul.

Money, greed, and power control people; they exalt themselves and hate their parents, especially if they are God-fearing parents, and try to steer them in the way of the Lord Jesus Christ.

All this is in the prophecy we see fulfilled in our lifetime.

God has placed those who understand the times here so we can warn others and be the light in a dark world with a message of hope, trusting in Jesus Christ, who will soon come and rescue His people from a dying and wicked world.

44

Signs & Warnings

Many people sense disorder and anarchy in the world. Maybe God is trying to get our attention before He brings Judgment down on the planet.

The Bible reveals God's methods as forewarning followed by swift retribution.

God sent Noah to forewarn humanity of His impending Judgment.

Sodom and Gomorrah were warned by angels of impending doom.

God dispatches His Watchmen and Women to forewarn of calamity coming.

He sent His prophets to forewarn the Israelites of impending doom, and He gave His faithful in this "church age" the "warning signs" of His wrath upon a God-rejecting world to warn others to escape the danger by turning to Jesus Christ, our only way of escape.

The scriptures tell us a day when the "warning signs" of a Seven-Year Tribulation will become a reality.

The ancient texts warn many times God will send His wrath in Judgment for the wickedness of humanity on earth.

The End Time signs globally are forewarning that impending doom is coming and should be taken seriously, and preparations must be made. Are you right with Jesus?

God told us to "watch" the signs so we will not be taken in the devil's trap; he has laid for all to fall in, primarily once the Rapture occurs; many will be caught in that trap.

Here is a list of some "vital" warning signs taking place even now:

- Antonio Guterres, the Secretary General of the United Nations, has advocated for the immediate and "global destruction" of the world's energy industry because fossil fuels are incompatible with human survival."
- Guterres emphasized the importance of a worldwide response. The fossil fuel sector is at the dirty center of climate catastrophe, so action in this area is urgently needed.

To paraphrase Guterres, "The world must phase out fossil fuels sustainably and equitably, moving to leave oil, gas, and coal in the earth where they originated from and dramatically increase green investment in a meaningful changeover."

Did you notice the words used by the Secretary-General? "A "global destruction" and "action" are needed in that area.

We use energy to sustain life by growing and shipping food to make it liveable for humanity. To cool and heat our dwellings, factories need production equipment. Our vehicles are made to transport us.

Think of the ramifications taken and human survival. These are "warning signs" in the making, and God is allowing us to hear the "warning bells" alerting us danger is imminent!

Another Warning

As mentioned, delegates from 193 nations met and approved a

document from the UN called "Transforming our World: the 2030 Sustainable Development Agenda."

That "covenant" became effective Jan1, 2016.

Simply, It calls for a global transition into global government by 2030—the Final World Empire.

General Guterres produced a progress report on the world government transition in early June 2023 and reported they are behind schedule.

The report claims that progress has slowed and that only seven years remain until the 2030 deadline has been missed.

It is roughly six and one-half years until 2030 from the date Guterres claimed in June 2023. It has many prophecy watchers on the alert because God said a Seven-Year covenant will be signed, and then the Tribulation begins.

Guterres stated that postponing or abandoning the goal of establishing a global government by 2030 is not a choice.

On September 18-19, 2023, the United Nations will host the SDG Summit to address this issue.

Additionally, the Feast of Trumpets (September 15-17) concludes on the day of the Summit.

Since the Jewish day begins the evening before the 18th (the first day of the SDG Summit) will not start until the evening of the 17th.

Ironically, the slogan for this SDG Summit is "A common call for leaving no one behind."

Isn't it a distorted version of the Rapture warning, satanically speaking?

September 21, 2023, will be celebrated as the International Day of Peace and corresponds with the SDG Summit.

According to the UN website, which emphasizes the importance of Peace and Security, 2023 represents the mid-point of the UN Sustainable Goals.

The Secretary-General hopes that world leaders will devote "seven years" of fast, sustained, and revolutionary action on a national and international scale to fulfill the SDGs (a global government established).

In other words, he is pushing for a "covenant" among world leaders to hasten the implementation of global governance by implementing more rapid changes over the following "seven years."

(Daniel 9:27) explains how the antichrist will confirm (make stronger, strengthen) a seven-year covenant.

We are not sure at this time how the covenant will be strengthened. There will be a rebellion briefly by three world leaders (Kings), and the Bible tells us the Antichrist will subdue them, and he will then be handed over total control over all the earth.

These warnings (signs) must be closely monitored as establishing an evil Final World Empire is nearing completion.

The Bible tells us the Antichrist cannot be revealed until after the restrainer (Holy Spirit) is taken out of the way, and that is when the "vanishing" of millions of people are caught up in the air to meet the Lord at that Blessed Hope.

I hope you are Ready!

45

Too Late for America

The United States of America is a sinful nation under God's Judgment.

God has raised many prophetic voices to urge America to repent and to warn that a nation ongoing in rebellion will bring about its destruction.

America has chosen to ignore the prophets sounding the warning. Instead, national resistance to God has hardened.

As a result, the nation has reached the end of its time to change from its evil ways and call out to God to free the country from condemnation.

Many Americans, including many Christians, reject the warnings of the truth. The Christian community leaves it because it has abandoned its principles for the world, hidden behind the banner of many different names, and fooled into thinking that its message of health, money, and happiness is universally applicable.

The people of Israel and Juda laughed at the prophets God had sent to call them to repentance.

They reminded the prophets, “Remember, we are God’s Chosen people. To paraphrase: God will never allow our nation to be destroyed. (Jeremiah 5:12-13. Micah 3:11).

God has called America to repent through His Watchmen and Women over several decades, yet, America has behaved like the ancient Israelites.

We have scoffed at the warnings by boastfully pointing out that we are a “Christian Nation,” which is no longer valid and has not been for quite some time.

America Under Judgment

In reality, we are far from a Christian Nation, as the country has taken on a Narcissistic behavior mannerism and mocks Christianity. Narcissism is Rising at an exceeding dangerous level in America!

Abortion, even up to birth and after, is something God will never ignore. Yet, this country is guilty of it.

Unnatural affection, going against God's laws, and nature is a grave abomination in His eyes, the scripture declares it, and this is why many bureaucrats plan to rewrite the scriptures, as mentioned, using Al. But who programs Al? Man does.

Mutilating young children is another severe and grave insult in the face of God; anyone taking part in such actions and supporting it will be held accountable.

Drug addiction, alcoholism, human trafficking, violent crime, gambling, child abuse, pornography, etc., is at an all-time high in the United States, making us the leader in such atrocities.

Furthermore, we portray our violent brand and rot to the world through such filth in films and TV shows.

America has poisoned the Earth morally more than any other nation.

We are reaping what we have sown as a result of our actions.

In America under Judgment, a cursed nation can be found in (Deuteronomy 28: 15-48).

The chapter points to a bleak picture of American society, with its cities in disarray, the youth in bondage, a confused and corrupt government, foreign policy in hiding, rampant diseases, families crumbling, ruined farms, and dominance by other countries increasingly more assertive.

Rebellion Rising

Nevertheless, we refuse to repent in the face of such condemnation. In reality, our resistance to God has hardened.

We have encouraged unnatural affection to be taught to young children, even pre-school, which is incomprehensible. Before it reached this point, handing out needles and condemns put the forces behind it on track for more depravity.

Every measure has been taken to protect every expression of obscenity and perversion in America.

As a result, society is taken over by blasphemies of every form as it scoffs at God and His principles here in America.

The United States turns its back on God as it thumbs its nose at His standards and ridicules those who try to adhere to His rules and laws.

The courts are in rebellion of God.

Congress no longer follows the guidelines set forth by the founders.

The powers that be want to remove God from all aspects of society and have done an excellent job thus far.

The educational system has banned God.

The United States Under God's Wrath

The terrorizing thing about a country with a behavior system such as America is when a nation that is already under Judgment, as we are currently, refuses to repent; ultimately, the reality is destruction.

God will soon remove the Judgments we are witnessing to impending doom.

The ancient text is plain at telling us this When such a dread release is overflowing, the country will not and cannot be spared, even if the righteous pray. (Ezekiel 14:12-20) tell us this.

The Final World Empire will result from America's demise and all its traditions, values, standards, and usual way of life people are familiar with.

While those behind the proponents of world dominance promise a world of peace, and you will be happy owning nothing, unable to travel anywhere, and still be happy, it is time to understand the severe consequences of what we as a country and the world are facing.

It is a communist form of government that they intend for humanity. It will make Starlin and Adolph Hitler's regimes look small in comparison.

I cannot stress enough; you don't have to be part of the people trapped in the deception of evil bureaucrats and left behind to face a world under God's wrath soon to fall during the Final World Empire.

Jesus died for you, even if you were the only person on earth; he loved you that much to free you from the dangerous time to come. He is waiting at the door of your heart to invite Him in. You must be the one to open that door to Him.

The Final World Empire is predicted to be the last form of government on earth when God's wrath falls on a God-rejecting world during the Tribulation, and then Jesus sets up the one true Kingdom; his Kingdom will last for 1,000 years, and you can be part of that, if you are right with Him, repent, ask Him to be Lord and Savior and live for Him.

It is not about a religion or a particular church but about Jesus; He is the "bridge" to the Father and no one or nothing else.

46

The UN's New Plan

To endorse a terrifying new plan allowing the United Nations to take jurisdiction over the entire planet in the event of a severe "culture disturbance" is on the agenda for just two months before the 2024 U.S. presidential election.

In the United States, most individuals do not know this is happening because the mainstream media are not covering it.

It should be front-page news nationwide, as many are now reporting it.

During "the Summit of the Future" in September 2024, world leaders will convene to adopt a "Pact for the Future."

The UN will organize a "Summit of the Future" two months before the presidential election, and this deal will reinforce the U.N.'s two-year-old Our Common Agenda policy revisions.

While many controversial proposals are on the agenda, perhaps none are as crucial as the United Nations' plan for a new "emergency platform."

It is a remarkable idea to give the United Nations sustainable powers in the event of future "worldwide culture disturbances," such as another universal pandemic, and it is possibly the most significant and aggressive idea on the agenda.

The official United Nations website provides detailed information about the "Summit of the Future" and the "Pact for the Future."

In typical UN fashion, the most disturbing aspects of their program are clocked in rhetoric about the world's need for peace, economic growth, and learning, among other things.

According to the UN's website, a stated goal of the "Summit of the Future" is implementing a more robust international response playbook for a complicated cultural disturbance, enhancing the use of the Secretary-General's convening power in the form of an Emergency Platform.

You may wonder what the "Emergency Platform" is they are talking about.

In March 2023, the UN published a policy report of disturbing details, and you can read about it on its website.

It wants the General Assembly to provide the Secretary-General and the United Nations system with standing authority to convene and operationalize an Emergency Platform in the event of a future complex culture disturbance of sufficient scale, severity, and reach.

As soon as it is activated, the emergency platform will provide the United Nations with the power to actively promote and drive an international response that places the principles of equity and solidarity at the center of its work.

To guarantee a coordinated global response to the crisis, the United Nations would convene all "stakeholders" worldwide, including academics, governments, actors from the private sector, and "international financial institutions."

To give the United Nations the power "to ensure there is a unified global response to the crisis" in the event of a giant "earth culture disturbance" is the worst possible scenario.

You may wonder what type of "culture disturbance" they are discussing.

According to the policy document, a future pandemic, a significant "event in outer space," or even "unforeseen risks" would qualify.

In my opinion, A significant event in outer space is what they suspect because the U.N. is not a Christian organization and never has been. Satan knows an important event is coming soon: the "vanishing" of millions of believers worldwide in the Harpaz Rapture of the church.

If Satan is aware, his followers are also mindful because they are under his influence.

Many different types of emergencies are listed in the policy report as potential causes for the emergency authority to be invoked. It includes" major climate events," future pandemic risks, a global digital connectivity disruption, major outer space events, and unforeseen risks.

It is to say, the question of whether to exercise these emergency powers is subject to different interpretations.

It has been discovered that the United Nations can keep prolonging these emergency powers forever after invoking them.

Although the duration of the emergency platform would initially be set for a "finite period," according to the United Nations' policy proposal, at the end of that period, the Secretary-General could extend the work of an Emergency Platform if required.

The UN would also receive the right to extend the emergency as they see fit.

Once implemented, the United Nations could remain influential over the situation indefinitely.

The One-World government promoters think this is fantastic, and this idea has previously received "multiple occasions" of official administrative support.

Officials have repeatedly supported the plan, leading many to question that "if the emergency platform is approved, the United States as we know it could cease to exist."

I know those with eyes to see and ears to hear are warning others how fast the prophecies are being fulfilled, as the "Tower of Babel" builders are speeding up their efforts to establish their Final World Empire, and then comes their leader, the Beast of Revelation 13, the Antichrist.

Summary of Goals to Establish World Government

The World Health Organization's Goals:

An International Code of Ethics.

A Worldwide Electronic Passport.

A Worldwide Electronic Currency.

A Worldwide Electronic Medical File.

The GDHCN Stands for a Global Digital Health Certification Network.

The World Economic Forum's Goals:

Artificially Created Holy Texts.

The IMF is Hoping for:

Data From Worldwide Electronic Transactions.

The UN Goals:

Everyone in the World to Have a Digital ID that is linked to a Bank Account.

An Agreement with Many People Throughout "Seven Years" to Establish a World Government, The Final World Empire.

The establishment of a global government and the beginning of the Tribulation Period is imminent unless God intervenes.

I pray that you take this very seriously and are not like the crowd in Noah's Day that ignored the Warnings.

47

CBDCs (Central Bank Digital Chip)

New information comes out every day on what the builders of the Final World Empire are doing in the completion of their establishing their World Government.

It is hard to keep up with so much information and then put it into print, but I am trying to keep readers up on the latest advancements in constructing the Agenda they are promoting.

This latest information is so critical that it brings the reality of what unfolds in a new light.

- In the not-too-distant future, all residents will need a Central Bank Digital Microchip (CBDC chip) implanted to access essential services like buying food and water.
- For citizens of the near future to access their bank accounts, they will be required to use the most up-to-date technology, a computer chip.

- It would help if you did not think about CBDCs as a form of currency but as a form of regulation (or permit system).
- At the moment, they are discussing a CBDC application for a mobile phone, but their end goal is to implant a chip under the skin of the users.

Please be aware that the World Economic Forum (WEF) intends very shortly for all citizens to have a chip implanted in their bodies.

Take Note; there is already a permit system in place for buying and selling.

People can engage in commercial activities after receiving the Mark of the Beast, a license (or permit) system.

To be able to buy and do business, individuals will be required to have a license or chip that bears the number (666), the name or mark of the Beast.

The Harpazo Rapture will probably occur at least three and one-half years before the Narcissistic World dictator and False Prophet require people to be chipped.

If that be the case, we are incredibly close to hearing the trumpet sound predicted by Jesus and the prophets and the "Blessed Hope" to take place.

In addition, I also discovered in researching this information that a possible manufactured economic catastrophe and subsequent efforts to force people to utilize a CBDC linked to an implanted chip under the skin.

Remember, when the chip (mark of the Beast) is implanted in people around the mid-point of the Tribulation, anyone who takes it will face impending doom when God's wrath falls, as well as the plagues that fall upon those who take it. There is no reversing it; once a person excepts the chip, (mark) Satan seals you.

Please be advised that under no circumstance ever take that mark!

48

Signs in the Heavens

Jesus foretold that "there shall be signs in the moon, sun, and stars, at the end of the age. (Luke 21:25).

The trajectories of three eclipses will merge to produce a massive "Aleph" over the United States, yet almost no one is aware of this phenomenon.

The first letter in the alphabet in Hebrew is Aleph.

The letter "Bet" comes in at position two in the Hebrew Alphabet.

The name "alphabet" was initially derived from combining the Hebrew letters Aleph and Bet.

The giant "Aleph" that will fall upon America is a remarkable expression from God in trying to get the attention of humanity, but only a few are aware.

It is why He tells us to "watch" so that we will be aware of His signs and warnings.

An eclipse can't occur without the sun and the moon's participation.

Hopefully, everyone remembers the August 21, 2017, Eclipse that started over Oregon, crossed the United States, and existed in South Carolina.

I live in South Carolina and experienced that extraordinary event as everyone was excited in that spiritual moment of watching God's handiwork and splendor.

The following Great Eclipse will occur on April 8, 2024, and begin on the East Coast, with a trajectory that will cross over; Maine, New Hampshire, Vermont, New York, Pennsylvania, Ohio, Indiana, Michigan, Tennessee, Kentucky, Oklahoma, Texas, and exist over Mexico.

When crossing makes a giant X over the country, parts of Kentucky, Illinois, and Missouri are located precisely at the junction of the Two Great Eclipses of 2017 and 2024.

Looking at the regions on the map more closely, you will notice that the junction point is smack dab amid the New Madrid Fault Zone.

New Madrid got its name from a small Missouri town called New Madrid.

The New Madrid fault line has triggered some of the most significant earthquakes ever recorded in the United States, and the aftershocks have been felt far away as 1,000 miles.

1811-1812 experienced such massive earthquakes in the New Madrid fault zone.

Losses above 3 billion and the displacement of over 2,000,000 people are possible outcomes of an earthquake of magnitude 7.7 along the New Madrid fault line.

The New Madrid Seismic Zone 3 poses the greatest threat of earthquakes in the United States anywhere besides the West Coast.

Yet another Eclipse will occur on October 14, 2023, crossing from Oregon to Texas.

If you place the route of that solar Eclipse on top of the pathway eclipse of 2017 and the one of April 8th, 2024, you will notice that these three eclipses combine to produce a massive "Aleph" across the United States.

First in the Hebrew alphabet is the letter Aleph. In Hebrew, the value of the Aleph is 1.

Additionally, the aleph symbolizes God and the unity of God, the only God.

Like the aleph, it consists of three lines—the whole of God's names: Father, Son, and Holy Spirit.

In the ancient text, the number three stands for the fullness of God.

The Aleph is from the old Hebrew writing system in Israel and Juda, where ancient inscriptions are found.

How does all this matter?

The new moon in Jerusalem in October 2023 falls on October 14th.

On the same day, the solar eclipse occurs and crosses the country from Oregon to Texas.

There is more:

The new moon in Jerusalem in April 2024 will occur on the 8th of April. Look it up on Google.

On the same day, the Great Eclipse will travel across the United States, thereby finishing the Aleph.

Furthermore, on the Hebrew calendar, the first day of the first month is the 8th of April, the first day of the year.

Simply, a New Biblical Year falls on that date.

I don't believe this is just by chance.

It is why God tells us; instead, He commands us to "watch."

He does not want anyone to be uninformed.

Additionally, I believe this to be one of the many signs in the heavens, as He told us events in the sun, moon, and stars will occur at the End of the Age. You can google and show the trajectory of the 2017 and 2024 solar eclipse on the US map. There you will see a giant X over the US that overlaps directly over the New Madrid faultline.

Are you watching?

49

The Millennial Reign of Jesus Christ

After the Tribulation ends, Jesus will return to establish His Kingdom rule for one-thousand years.

According to Revelation 19 and 20, the thousand-year reign of this Kingdom will be followed by eternal life in the new world God will create.

During the thousand years, also known as the Millenium, Jesus will unite Heaven and Earth under His rule. (Ephesians 1:10).

In What Ways Will the Planet Change?

Before the Lord's Kingdom reign, God will remove the curse He placed on the globe after the fall of Adam and Eve and restore the planet. (Isaiah 11:34-35, Micah 4, Zechariah 8-14).

Before the Millennial reign of Jesus, the planet underwent a dramatic change; it was after the Tribulation Period. (Revelation 16:18-19).

When the Lord returns, a massive earthquake will split the city of Jerusalem into three sections; it is when Christ's feet touch the ground on the Mount of Olives, and water will begin to flow out of Jerusalem. (Zechariah 14:4-8).

Over this river will be built the new temple lasting a thousand years. (Ezekiel 47:1-12).

During Jesus' rule, Jerusalem will be the highest point on the entire planet.

The remaining land on earth will consist of small hills here and there.

(Revelation 16:20 and Isaiah 40:4-5) tell us that the tremendous earthquake that will accompany the Return of Christ at the end of the Tribulation will level the mountains of the earth, and the islands will disappear, as mentioned in a previous chapter.

The weather patterns on Earth are significantly influenced by the presence of mountains.

Eliminating mountains will improve the state of the planet's climate; it will be more serene.

During the Kingdom reign of the Messiah, only one mountain will stand, and the city of Jerusalem will be placed on the top of that mountain where Jesus and His saints will live.

Mortal Humans Will Continue to Exist

During the thousand-year reign, the bible indicates that mortal humans will continue to exist.

New converts who make it through the Tribulation will enter the Millennial Kingdom, where they and their offspring will live forever under Jesus' authority.

The ancient texts tell us Jesus will rule with a "rod of iron."

The prophecy explains that the reign of Christ will be characterized by "Justice and Judgment."

For this reason, His rule will be just, and punishment will be speedy and severe, ruling with a "rod of iron" Read (Micah 4:3).

In the Kingdom, the Lord will swiftly punish those who rebel, and peace will rule (Isaiah 9:6-7).

What the Raptured Saints and Those Who Have Died in Christ Will Do During the Kingdom is Clarified Below:

- The righteous will share the Kingdom and rule. (Daniel 7:18-27).
- The righteous shall sit as officers, judges, and magistrates.
- The new convert believers will learn from the saints. (Psalm 37:29-31).

The Martyred Saints

A specific place as servants in God's temple will be reserved for those who were martyred during the Tribulation by the Antichrist regime (Revelation 20:6), and those who make it through the Tribulation unharmed will be appointed as the local governors and mayors of the Kingdom. (Luke 19:16-19, Matthew 25:23).

The New Jerusalem, The Dwelling Place of the Saints

The New Jerusalem is in Heaven; you can read it in Revelation 21, 22. It is where the Raptured saints reside and all those who died before the Rapture up unto the Millenium Reign. It is the permanent residence of the saints, even though they will govern and reign from Earth during the Millennium.

Many prophecy scholars believe the New Jerusalem (the Golden City) will be visible from Earth.

It will be like a planet in orbit around the Earth. Because the Raptured saints and those who died in Christ before the Millennium received their "glorified bodies," they can travel from Earth to the New Jerusalem as they desire.

Human Lifespan Will Increase

As a result of God removing the curse from the earth, human lifespan will increase to levels as they did before the flood.

Those born during the thousand-year reign of Jesus Christ will have a century to decide whether or not to accept Jesus as the Lord and Savior.

If they refuse Jesus and continue to live in sin, they will not live a longer life, and it also means that those who follow Jesus will be immune to physical death. (Isaiah 65:20).

The Reason for the Millennium

It was promised to Abraham by God and to his descendants.

Jesus was promised a Kingdom where He would rule and reign with His people. (Genesis 15:18-21, Ezekiel 47:13-17).

The Millenium is also for God to test the Jewish people and others to see if they will faithfully serve Him (Revelation 20:1-3).

It is also a time of peace and harmony where the righteous enjoy spending time in the Kingdom with their beloved Messiah, Jesus Christ.

50

Be Ready

The Rapture is approaching, and we should all ensure we are prepared to meet the Lord when the Trumpet sounds.

Getting ready for the Rapture is much less complicated than you might believe.

To summarize, you must accept Jesus as your personal Savior by sincerely repenting your sins and asking Him to come into your heart.

He stands at the door of your heart knocking, but you must open that door by saying yes, to Him, and He will come in. It is a choice each of us must make if we want to be forgiven and spend eternity with Him and be ready for the Rapture.

The Rapture is reserved for all Born-Again believers and is predicted in (1 Thessalonians 4:15-18).

Remember, Paul is addressing the above verse to those who have said "Yes" to Jesus; they are prepared and have the promise of that "Blessed Hope," known as the Harpaz Rapture.

Those who have not accepted the Lord's invitation and reject the "gift" of salvation the Lord offers them by the Lord dying on the cross and shedding His blood for them will not participate in that "Blessed Event." As a result, that day will come upon them, as the Lord describes, "as a thief in the night." (1 Thessalonians 5:2). They will be caught off guard when that day finally arrives.

Those left behind will face the horrors of the Tribulation Period but choose to do so after hearing the Truth. They will be without excuse, and sadly, they will face impending doom.

Because of their faith, those that have accepted the "gift" Jesus offers, and have said "yes" to Him, are the Born-Again believers that are the five prudent virgins spoken of in (Matthew 25:1-3) that have their lamps trimmed and lit as they watch and wait for the Lord's return.

When Jesus does return, the vast majority of humanity will not have that faith, ushering in an era of spiritual complacency and rejection of the Son of God.

Will you be part of the group that will soon hear the trumpet sound and the Lord's voice calling you?

According to {John 10:14; 14:1-3) Jesus will return for those He claims to be His. He knows you by name.

Don't be left to face the darkest time in history, when millions will die because of the impending release of God's wrath to fall on all those that rejected His Son Jesus Christ during the time known as the Tribulation Period, living under the Final World Empire ruled by a Narcissistic, Satanic world dictator, the Antichrist.

Jesus is our only hope; there is none other. He is the bridge to the Father.

The prophecies that warn us of events in End Times are everywhere, converging rapidly, just as predicted by Jesus Himself.

The Final World Empire builders are racing to complete their goal of Agenda 2030, the Great Reset, the One-World Government.

You only have one chance to accept the One who died and shed His blood for you so you don't spend eternity without Him.

Whether or not you believe the things written in this book does not matter. They will come to pass. I pray you say yes to Jesus; your name will be written in the Book of Life.

God Bless You!

51

Epilogue - July 2023

The world is in chaos after the Rapture, and the Final World Empire has finally arrived, ushing in the Tribulation Period predicted by the prophets and Jesus Himself.

The Antichrist, known as the Beast of Revelation 13, will sign a Seven-Year Covenant with the Jewish people and others.

It will seem as if all is lost during this time, and the Narcissistic World Leader will appear to have all the answers, uniting all humanity under a false persona.

Deception will run rampant under the Final World Empire, as the Tower of Babel builders will

finally, have the Utopia they so much desired.

But will it be what they want?

The "vanishing" of millions of people on earth in the Rapture will be a New Beginning for those who have long awaited their Lord's Return.

After the Millennial reign of Christ, God will release Satan and his fallen angels from the bottomless pit, and he will encircle the camp of the righteous to try and destroy them.

God will send fire down upon him, and he will forever spend eternity in the Lake that burns with fire and brimstone, where the Antichrist and False Prophet are.

All who rejected Christ will spend Eternity in the Lake of Fire.

The New Jerusalem will be on earth, and at the same time, a New Heaven and Earth will be created by God, where Jesus and all the saints will live in eternity.

About The Author

Lori Buelow has studied Eschatology for over four decades. Her previous outreach programs on social media, different Websites, and most recent one, Light House News and More.org; as well as founder and organizer of a small church in Germany on a military base where her husband served; and writing, have all been part of her ministry in reaching the lost for Jesus Christ.

Raised in a mainline denomination and never heard about a One-World Government formed by a ruthless leader, the Antichrist, during the Final World Empire. One day she listened to a message about this by Billy Graham and Salvation by Grace only through Jesus; Lori knew this was what she had missed most of her life. Now as a Born-Again believer, she wants to tell others about those events the Prophets and Jesus Himself warned would come to pass.

The Author loves spending time outdoors with her husband, and pet dog, Nacho, and enjoys hiking, cycling, beach, mountains, and gardening.

www.ingramcontent.com/pod-product-compliance
Ingram Content Group UK Ltd.
Pitfield, Milton Keynes, MK11 3LW, UK
UKHW020419250726
13967UKWH00007B/2725